Rein In Your Brain

Endorsements for *Rein In Your Brain*

"Rarely do writers reveal such a transparent look into how they personally survived the overwhelming life circumstances that led to the creation of a practical and profound way of healing and change for the rest of us. And it's for everyone— from the professional counselor or educator to the shattered person recovering from addiction and childhood trauma. A must-read for all who have waited for a genuine, real-world application of the valuable truths revealed in brain research."

—Jean M. LaCour, Ph.D., founder/CEO of NET Institute,
Rise Professional Recovery Coaching

"Having been a major advocate in the field of addiction treatment and recovery, Cynthia Moreno Tuohy, and her colleague Victoria Costello, have written an empowering book that allows the reader to take another significant step in their recovery. You will better understand both the behavior and its underpinnings that keep you emotionally and relationally stuck in recovery while being given a plethora of tools to practice that will move you forward. Congratulations to the authors for offering a major contribution to our field."

—Claudia Black, Ph.D., author of *It Will Never Happen to Me*

"I have rarely come across a book that is as well written, insightful, and filled with practical exercises that can benefit us all. *Rein In Your Brain* is a must-read for anyone interested in the heart and science of improving their relationships!"

—Rokelle Lerner, clinical director, InnerPath workshops

"*Rein In Your Brain* is inspirational, informative, and filled with simple yet profound suggestions to change from living a life filled with impulsive, instinctual reactions to one marked by reflective, respectful responding. Cynthia Moreno Tuohy is a recovery 'thriver,' not just a survivor. Her own recovery story that she courageously shares is filled with life and relationship lessons and wisdom. Anyone who has struggled with dysfunctional actions, emotional reactions, and relationships will be able to connect with and learn from the 'Ten Big Ideas' she describes. They offer practical, psychologically sound, and sophisticated advice and strategies that can change lives. The book is filled with helpful self-assessments and suggestions to recover from our automatic, self-defeating, 'limbic' reactions and sense of loss of control with a goal of building a life filled with peace, passion, and purpose that respects both self and other. Though they are easier to read than to incorporate into our lives, Cynthia's Ten Big Ideas offer wonderful ways to support recovery and wellness."

—Dr. Carlo DiClemente, ABPP, Presidential Research Professor
of Psychology at University of Maryland, Baltimore County,
and cocreator of the transtheoretical (stages of change) model

Rein In Your Brain

*From Impulsivity to
Thoughtful Living in Recovery*

Cynthia Moreno Tuohy, BSW, NCAC II,
with Victoria Costello

Hazelden
Publishing

Hazelden Publishing
Center City, Minnesota 55012
hazelden.org/bookstore

Library of Congress Cataloging-in-Publication Data

Tuohy, Cynthia Moreno.
  Rein in your brain : from impulsivity to thoughtful living in recovery /
Cynthia Moreno Tuohy and Victoria Costello.
    pages cm
  ISBN 978-1-61649-467-4 (paperback) — ISBN 978-1-61649-503-9 (ebook)
  1. Substance abuse—Treatment. 2. Addicts—Rehabilitation.
  3. Addicts—Psychology. I. Costello, Victoria. II. Title.
  HV4998.T86 2014
  616.86'03—dc23

                                                         2013044761

Editor's note
The names, details, and circumstances may have been changed to protect the
privacy of those mentioned in this publication.

 This publication is not intended as a substitute for the advice of health care
professionals.

 Alcoholics Anonymous and AA are registered trademarks of Alcoholics
Anonymous World Services, Inc.

26 25 24 23 22 2 3 4 5 6

Cover design: Theresa Jaeger Gedig
Interior design: Kinne Design
Typesetting: BookMobile Design and Digital Publisher Services

To my children, Rudy Moreno and Chelsea Mikel, who evidenced the change in our family and are amazing adults whom I love and respect. My children have grown up influenced by the Big Ideas in this book, and today they lead a much different life of wellness in relationships than the generation that birthed them. I am grateful to their fathers for giving me such beautifully spirited children and for teaching me lessons that assisted my growth, both personally and professionally.

To my current husband, Christopher Tuohy, who has been a cheerleader as the work on this book was growing and changing, just as in the seasons that it took to write, through the sun, rain, and snow.

✧

*"Whatever games are played with us, we must
play no games with ourselves, but deal
in our privacy with the last honesty and truth."*

— RALPH WALDO EMERSON

Contents

Acknowledgments

Today, and every day, I am deeply grateful to my family of origin and the life given to me, the lessons learned and relearned, and the passion in my inner being, my soul, and my heart to work with individuals and families yet to be in recovery, which resulted from my life experiences. I'm also grateful for and honored by the clients who have given me the opportunity to work with them, some now in almost thirty years of recovery and others working to achieve that first beginning of recovery. I'm always and in all ways reminded how insidious the diseases of addiction are, how powerful the recovery process is, and of the synergy of people loving people to take those first and ongoing steps in the process of change.

Addiction recovery is a lifelong process. Trauma recovery is also a lifelong process. We all are in recovery from something—just living in this fast-paced world of "get it done, do it well, be something or someone" brings huge stress to the persons we are inside the shell we wear daily. This book is meant to bring hope—hope for recovery in addiction, trauma, life! Without hope, there is no light to recovery.

There are thousands of addiction counselors, educators, and other professionals whom I have had the extreme pleasure to work with in some capacity. They are my heroes and colleagues—I treasure them. Many addiction counselors and other helping counselors have been trained in the *Rein In Your Brain* concepts and life patterns of change. They are in communities around the globe, ready to assist you in your growth and change process. At NAADAC, the Association for Addiction Professionals, we train and support counselors to use these tools to serve others. These counselors carry the hope of recovery and the belief that change is possible. Please connect with them when you need more professional support and guidance. They are "earth angels"!

My colleagues at NAADAC, the Association for Addiction Professionals, our executive committee, and leadership have given me a place to grow and belong for more than thirty years. They have become my extended family and support group. It is important for all of us to find an environment that will nurture us and help us develop—and for many of you that will be your church, temple, mosque, tribe, Twelve Step group, and other support groups. It is important to lean toward those with whom you can connect and grow. My prayer is that you find this connection if you have not already.

We all have families, and I am blessed to have my older sister, Kathy, and brother, Jess, still in my life. In my adult years, reconnecting with my four half-siblings has been a wonderful addition to my life. It has not been easy for Jeffrey, Mary Margaret ("Tiny"), Greg, and Rhett to connect to a family from which they were distanced in many ways. They have shared beautiful stories of our father, Jess, and the love we all share for him is immeasurable. It, too, is a lifelong process to recover the family that was shattered. In the process of family reconstruction, my stepfather, Cliff, and his wife, Judith, have entered heart and soul to help us reclaim the positive and beautiful stories of our mother, Doris. And they brought with them Victoria—the person who collaborated with me on this book. Her expertise, wisdom, and commitment to this book boosted my belief in the reality of this book. To Mom and Pop Bickford, who loved us, and loved us the best they knew how. To Ann and Dwight—my foster parents—and their daughters, for raising me up: physically, emotionally, psychologically, and spiritually. Without your intervention and continued support, I believe my life would have ended long ago.

Hazelden has been an organization that I have learned from for many years, from the treatment model to their education programs, and I am thrilled that our paths have crossed on this book.

A special dedication to Chuck DeVore, M.A., who taught me about anger management and conflict resolution, gave me some of his materials and his vision, and then died, suddenly, before he could assist me as cowriter. His words, teachings, and spirit live on in this book. I believe he is smiling in heaven, happy to know that others will be touched by the work that we meant to build and share with each of you, together. His wife, Gwen, is the other lovely gift he left behind, and I am grateful to have her supporting me in this work.

So, we don't know what we don't know, and I did not know where my Higher Power was taking me when I began this journey in my family of origin. My belief is that nothing is wasted, not any of the trauma or difficulties. My hope for you as you read is that you integrate and pass it on!

Blessings,
Cynthia

Introduction

At every age, people learn best by example. This is why religious texts use parables and stories to teach important lessons, like the Good Samaritan who helps a stranger, or Job who never gives up no matter what awfulness comes his way—and so on. In the same way, this talent for imitation is why the behaviors our parents teach us early—when our brains are most impressionable—stick with us throughout our lives. This is either good news or not so good news, depending on how well your parents steered their own lives and how much they taught you about being a responsible driver of your own.

As the youngest of my parents' three children, I became a ward of the state at the age of eight months. By fifteen, I'd been in and out of forty homes. With no stable family of my own, I counted on alcohol and drugs, my peers, and a budding career in petty crime to sustain me and soothe my pain.

How and why did my parents allow such terrible things to happen to my siblings and me? My mother and father were intelligent and well-intentioned people who—because they'd never been shown a better way to handle their impulses, and inherited vulnerabilities to alcohol and drug addiction—lurched from one experience to another, exerting little self-control and even less reflection on their actions. As a result, they often made their own lives miserable, and they did a dreadful job of raising us.

My life story is worse than many, although not as bad as others. In this book, I share some of the difficult experiences I faced as a child and adolescent to demonstrate how hard times can lead to the negative habits of mind and behavior that so many of us in recovery confront in ourselves and others. These episodes of abuse, neglect, despair, and loneliness forced me to learn certain tough lessons very early in life. Other people may face similar trials well into their adulthoods, for example, when relationships, family strife, or financial devastation create chaos in their lives.

Regardless of when they occur, such trips to the edge of what we think we can possibly bear can also be a catalyst to push us in a new direction. Perhaps a loss or major disappointment has led you to explore a new path at this time and place in your life! If so, welcome! I invite you to think of this book as a GPS, a handy device sending you a steady stream of directions to guide you through the process of leaving fear-driven, self-defeating thoughts and behaviors in the past. I promise, if you proceed step by step, in the course of this journey, you will uncover a new and happier you—not someone who is foreign to you, but a version of yourself that has been there all along, hiding behind a lifetime of negative habits.

Like many people struggling with addiction, I was saved from a life of misery through daily acts of self-care and participation in a community of people committed to their own recovery. I've also spent three decades as a practicing addiction counselor and, more recently, working with addiction professionals as both a trainer and an advocate for our profession. And yet, like many of you, even as I talk the talk and walk the walk of recovery, I still occasionally experience frustration when those old negative habits of mind sneak back in and "make me" revert to self-destructive ways of thinking and being—everything I associate with addiction and the pain that came before I accepted the help of others who've traveled this route before me and shared their lessons.

You'll note the term *addict* is nowhere to be found in the previous paragraph. I prefer to use "person in recovery" or any other phrase emphasizing the process of recovery. This helps reduce the stigma attached to the term *addict*. *Addiction* in this book refers to a variety of addictive substances and patterns, among them alcohol and drugs, sex and pornography, food, gambling, and addictive relationships.

Through my ongoing study of the "science of addiction and recovery," and, after talking with and training thousands of my professional peers, I've distilled from addiction recovery what I call the "Ten Big Ideas" and put them into a self-help format for easy use by recovering people and their families. Let me be the first to say, these are not brand-new ideas; to the contrary, each of these Ten Big Ideas is a tried-and-true concept adapted from the addiction recovery and social work professions. Some or all of them are being used by addiction professionals in counseling and treatment centers, and by individuals in self-help and community-based programs around the world.

This experiential approach is designed to help anyone, and especially those already committed to sobriety, make the next leap in addiction recovery. Many of these concepts will feel intuitively "right on" to you, but may seem too difficult to apply in your day-to-day life. I encourage you to try to stick with it. The exercises illustrating each Big Idea are designed to show you how to replace the old fear-driven habits of impulsivity that can stay long after the "substance" is gone with the new habits of a thought-based way of life.

I devote a chapter to each Big Idea, explaining what it means and how it works in "real life." I'll share my own experiences and the personal stories of people I've worked with as a counselor and trainer. I'll also share some fictional vignettes, which illustrate what happens when we confront impulsive words and actions in ourselves and others, and I'll encourage you to try out new ways of thinking and behaving.

Before we dive into the Ten Big Ideas, I present a very brief lesson in neuroscience. Simply put, in order to rein in our impulses, we must get to know our brains better. The insights I share come from the latest advances in brain imaging and from the work of cognitive psychologists. Their work sheds light on exactly how our brains can lead us down the "wrong" path, and how our capabilities for rational thought and self-control can help us reverse course.

It sounds like heady stuff (pun intended)! While the science may appear highly technical, the solution to ending old counterproductive behaviors is often as simple as using mindfulness techniques to gain self-awareness and employing different words and phrases to express everyday thoughts and feelings. If you give the Big Ideas and exercises the opportunity to work, you can and will make profound changes in your life. While most of my examples refer to intimate relationships (dating, marriage, etc.), the Big Ideas can be applied in almost any relationship (coworkers, relatives, children, etc.).

To begin the process of understanding and learning how to work the Ten Big Ideas, I ask that you open your heart and mind to whatever resonates from the factual information, vignettes, and personal stories to come. You will find it useful to keep a pen and paper nearby. Sometimes family photos can also help jog your memory about "how it was" when you were growing up, or help you recall what transpired in an earlier relationship. Remember that each person brings a different life script to this endeavor. That means each of us will take a slightly different path in our journey through recovery.

Ten Big Ideas from Addiction Recovery

- Stand Still in the Moment (and back up the train)
- Do Not Assume Intent (take away the blame game)
- Dig Deeper into the Conflict (discover)
- Cultivate Confusion (remove the wall of misunderstanding)
- Understand the Paradox of Control (see that it's not necessary to control)
- Dismantle the Wall of Misunderstanding (get not to my truth or your truth, but *our* truth)
- Create a Blameless Relationship with Yourself
- Avoid Premature Forgiveness (go beyond "Whew! I'm off the hook")
- Put Down Your Dukes
- Take Responsibility for Self-Fulfilling Prophecies (know your past, change your future)

After working these concepts with thousands of people in clinical treatment and in workshops around the world, I see the fallout that results from unchecked impulsivity as a nearly universal challenge. I've also seen and heard with my own eyes and ears how, if you let yourself go into the heart of each idea and try the exercises offered in each chapter, you will be much closer to a level of fulfillment you've only ever dreamed about before.

Blessings,
Cynthia

The Beginnings of a Life
Lived in the Limbic

The only way we can change the future—for ourselves, our children, and our grandchildren—is to accept who we are in the present. To make meaningful changes to our present thoughts and behaviors, we must also understand the forces from the past that shaped us. Beginning in this chapter, and in bits and pieces throughout the book, I offer my personal journey as a way to illustrate the Ten Big Ideas. You'll also find exercises for reining in your brain and finding a more thoughtful way to live in recovery.

At each juncture, my hope is that you'll reflect on not only how our life experiences may be similar (or different), but also on how the hurts and hard lessons in any life can produce limiting and painful habits of mind and behavior. By witnessing each other's wounds and owning our own, we can untie the ropes of habit and begin to walk into a less fettered future.

My Story

My mother, Doris, gave birth to me, her third child, at age nineteen. When I was born, she and my father, Jess, lived in a working-class part of Walla Walla, in Western Washington State. In the first of countless family disruptions and breakups initiated by my mother's reckless actions, she took off when I was less than a year old. She left without a word of explanation, and with no note or phone call to explain her disappearance, leaving my father to wonder if she'd been kidnapped or killed. He would eventually learn that Doris intentionally deserted him. And she did it to have a shot at realizing her dream of being on the stage—an ambition that took her a thousand miles away to Miami, Cuba, and Southern California.

To say that Doris was uninterested in the role of mother is only partly true. Sporadically, she wanted it desperately and would reassert her maternal rights to pull me out of whatever situation I'd landed in since her last exit. I suspect Doris's returns occurred more because she found it socially difficult to admit she wasn't capable of being a mother, rather than out of any real sense of duty. My mother, who suffered from largely untreated bipolar disorder, had other priorities. Among them, she hoped to become a dancer, an actress, or a model, and live unencumbered in her addictions.

A Family Living in the Limbic

My father's response to his wife's desertion was to drink—a lot. It was his way of dealing with conflict and myriad life circumstances that were no longer working for him. Given his time and place, what else did he know to do? Neither he, nor anyone of his generation, understood that as human beings we are capable of "reining in" impulsive actions emanating from our "limbic brains."

If you're not accustomed to reading about brain research or science, please don't panic about my use of unfamiliar scientific words or concepts. Although neuroscience (the study of how our brains work) is more popularly discussed today, understanding the difference between impulse versus thought-based behaviors and their connection to opposite parts of the brain is a much newer area. I'll get into much more detail about how the limbic system feeds impulsive behavior and how these more extreme tendencies can be reined in by the cortex, or "thinking brain," in the next chapter. For now, suffice it to say that the instincts emanating from our limbic brain take over our thoughts and actions when we're faced with the pain of abandonment or any other perceived threat to our sense of security.

At times like those, the ancient "mammalian" part of your brain steps in to prepare you for "fight or flight." Our ancient ancestors depended on their fight-or-flight instincts for survival. We've all had such moments—when we feel as if a twenty-foot-tall wooly mammoth is barreling down toward us, and we have no way out. If one were to judge by the limbic-driven, impulsive behaviors of my parents and other "role models" in my early life, it might have seemed like my family had been constantly surrounded by a herd of stampeding mammoths. In fact, it was simply the day-to-day challenge of work, raising children, and maintaining adult relationships that undid the adults in my world.

In the wake of my mother's departure, and my father's emotional unraveling, other family members helped out as much as they could with housekeeping and childcare. But when minding three little kids became too much for everyone, we were moved to a group home in Moses Lake. And, with this first move, I began serving an eighteen-year sentence as a ward of the state, a child under the care and control of the court and foster care system.

I don't know how long we stayed at the Moses Lake facility or how much time passed in each of the many foster and family homes and group situations following that first placement. Until puberty, my memory consists mainly of fragments of frequently dramatic, sometimes violent, events ending one situation and leading to another.

My mother's inconsistency about what she wanted, or could handle, as a parent probably made my childhood worse than it would have been had she simply left for good. I'm told that some thirty-three months after she first took leave, my mother returned in person, asking my father if she could see her children for a few hours. My father, so grateful to lay eyes on the woman he still loved and so missed, gave in. But she never made it back to his house that day. Instead, as soon as she put us in the car, we took off for Los Angeles.

It did not take long for the responsibilities of parenting to conflict with her career as a sometime dancer and model, and her struggle with addiction. Less than six months after taking us, she called my father and asked him to come get us. Once we were back in Washington State, it then didn't take long for him to realize he couldn't handle us either—so off we went to another home. At this point, to our great relief, the paternal grandparents we called "Mom" and "Pop" stepped in and asked the state to give them custody, taking the three of us into their home. At this point I was four years old.

Maybe it was Doris's finding out that we were living with her disapproving former in-laws that led to the next upheaval. Soon after we were settled in with our grandparents, she filed in court to get custody back for herself. I have vivid memories of the court hearing where this battle played out: my brother, sister, and I sitting in the back of an immense courtroom listening to the muffled voices of both our parents as they made their cases to a judge. Once they sat down, the judge asked for a private audience with the three of us kids. From the combative courtroom, we were escorted to his cozy, wood-paneled chambers, where I immediately felt safer. To my surprise, the judge seemed genuinely interested in our opinions of our parents, and he asked whom we would choose to live with. All three of us were of the same mind. We didn't want to go back to either of them; we wanted to live with our grandparents, "Mom" and "Pop." The judge smiled and gave us each a lollipop before we were ushered back to the courtroom to hear his verdict. I remember feeling so happy and relieved.

But the verdict was not what I expected. The judge announced that we were going back to the sole custody of our mother. We would be leaving with her—immediately. And then he hammered his gavel and left. I couldn't understand what had just happened. Instinctively, I screamed and held onto the bench when my mother tried to take me by the hand and lead me away. My brain was already telling me this was trouble, and my survival depended on fighting to remain with my grandparents. Even if the judge didn't know it, at four years old, I was absolutely certain that Mom and Pop were the only sane and stable adult figures in my life.

No matter. Off we went in a yellow convertible with my mother and Cliff, the attorney who by then had become the man in her life, back to LA to live in isolation from the family we knew and loved. You will not be surprised to learn that this new situation didn't last long. Mother blew it up with her drugging, drinking, and cheating. Nonetheless, her court victory had me relocated to Southern California, which became my home for nearly a decade. It was there that several significant things happened to me—most of them no good.

It's not hard to imagine how so much chaos shapes a young heart and brain, and how a child's brain moves to protect itself from the resulting stress and pain. Not having a home or parent figure for a sustained period of time damaged my sense of self and any notion of security or trust I might have developed. Abandonment became my middle name. Having no sense of personal power or control in life left me feeling powerless. Later, being physically and sexually abused caused me to feel worthless and incapable of defending myself—and so I compensated by becoming tough on the outside. On the inside, however, I was a sad and hurt little girl.

Tough on the Outside

When I entered puberty, I started running with other kids who were doing the same insane things that I was doing to make my life seem more manageable, like turning to drugs and petty crime. I became such an expert at the deviant life that, by age eleven, I formed my own girl-gang. Actually, I thought of us more as a girlie-girl club—girls doing whatever it took to take care of ourselves.

My probation officer at the time first used the term *juvenile delinquents* to describe my friends and me. Looking back, I can see that the other girls and I were like laboratory rats running on treadmills, keen on receiving a coveted reward. We chased our highs on a daily basis by skipping school, drinking, and taking drugs regularly—any kind of drug. We sniffed glue, binge-drank, and eventually graduated to using speed. We were also physically tough and got very good at beating up other teenagers, including boys.

Before long, my girlfriends and I became master thieves and fencers of stolen goods—with a method to our madness. We would go into fancy department stores to study the layout, and then plan how to tear through and take as much jewelry as we could. Then we'd sell what we stole to other kids. Most of the time, I'd use the money I made shoplifting to buy food and clothes, sometimes sharing my bounty with my brother, Jess (named after our father). By this point in puberty, I'd developed rickets, a result of poor nutrition and, most likely, my early drug use. I craved fruit, milk, and other foods we weren't getting at home, so I used the money to buy them.

Where were the authority figures in my life during this time? The caseworkers and probation officers assigned to me never saw my potential. They missed the fact that it took great organizational and leadership skills, as well as creativity, to do all that I was doing just to survive. So did the teachers and principals at my elementary and junior high schools, who never seemed to notice the pain I was in, or how it was shaping my behavior. They didn't understand that I needed to inflict my pain on others, just as I felt it was being inflicted on me.

My father moved back to Southern California from Washington State to be closer to his kids. It was in Southern California that my father remarried. The woman he married, Peggy, quickly gave birth to two children of their own. Unfortunately, my father had not learned from the mistake he'd made marrying my mother, and it wasn't long before this became evident. Peggy was just as troubled and dangerous as my mother—in her own way.

My mother, having split from her husband Cliff, had a difficult time making it on her own. She would get desperate with managing three children and ship me off to some "aunt and uncle," who were not relatives but friends, to substitute for parents. When these living arrangements didn't work, I ended up with my father and Peggy.

In another stunning rerun of his first marriage, Peggy ran away. There was my father, abandoned again, feeling unbearable pain. No doubt, memories of past hurt and rejection came flooding back to his brain, and his mammalian limbic brain once again engaged in a fight for survival. Soon, we were all on our way back to Washington State to find Peggy and the babies.

Trying Again to Be a Family

With all of us once more in Washington State, my father and Peggy reconciled, and things were quiet as we worked to settle into a new house. It was a tight squeeze with four of us kids sharing one bedroom: Jess, the two babies, and me. My sister Kathy had gone to Washington State to live with our mother. (Mother had a way of keeping my older sister with her and leaving my brother and I to fend for ourselves.) However, the change in location did little to reduce the patterns of abuse, denial (on my father's part, about marrying another unstable woman, as well as his drinking), and the acting out that had already become my modus operandi.

Home life quickly deteriorated. Terrible fights ensued between Peggy and me. Peggy had her own way of trying to control me and my life. She would have me care for her babies, clean house, and cook after getting home from school, and then just before my father was due to arrive home, she would begin to beat me for not "doing what I was supposed to do." My father would walk in the door to this chaos, not knowing what to do for fear that if he tried to interfere, she would leave with his new set of babies. There were times when the scratches were so deep on my arms and back, and the hair pulled from roots, that blood was running in several directions. I would run from the house looking for someone to care and protect me from the craziness in which we lived.

Finally, after one fight too many, I ran away from their house and refused to go back. And once again, my paternal grandparents took me in. Sometime later, on my urging, they also brought Jess—who had been farmed out again to foster care—to come live with us.

In the summer of my fifteenth year, things had finally reached something like calm in my grandparents' home with my brother Jess and me. Unsurprisingly, that was exactly when my mother stepped back in to destabilize us all over again. At the beginning of that summer, she invited Jess and me to spend a month with her and my sister, Kathy, on the west side of Washington State. Why she thought having us with her was a good idea, it's hard to say. It's likely she wasn't thinking much at all. In a short time, her daily regimen—crystal meth, with a cocktail of booze and barbiturates to help her come down—soon became ours. We were children modeling what we thought was the "cool way" to be.

This is a common dynamic when the so-called grown-ups in a household abdicate the responsibilities of adulthood. Little or no thought is given to child development or age-appropriate behaviors. These adults live each day to the fullest—with a single-minded goal to meet their need to get high, in whatever way works or is available to them at the time.

Many of us who become addicted in adolescence are mimicking these parental behaviors. Part of our later pain comes from feeling neglected and abandoned by mothers and fathers who weren't there for us. The habit of self-medicating this kind of pain then becomes habituated as a defensive coping mechanism.

I recall waking up after a month of living this lifestyle and feeling sick from whatever I'd ingested the night before. I walked through the living room to the kitchen and saw the same disgusting mess—dirty dishes and clothing, old newspapers, layers of dust, and dying plants—everywhere. It dawned on me that this was a very dangerous life for my brother and me to be living, even though our mother was at the center of it. I went and found Jess and said, "We need to do something different or we'll turn out just like her."

"What should we do?" he asked.

"I'm not sure," I said. But then an idea came to me. "Maybe we should go to that church . . . you know, the one with the youth group in the building where Pop did the stone work." However illogical, I thought that if my grandfather had worked there, that church must be a good and safe place to be.

My brother's eyebrows shot up.

"Church?" he said, pointing out that it was not our "usual" habit to attend church. "So why now?" he wanted to know.

I couldn't explain it. I just knew that hooking up with that church in my grandparents' town was the only way out of the downward spiral we had fallen into with our mother.

So, a few days after getting back to Mom and Pop's house, Jess and I joined the youth group run by a nice couple, Ann and Dwight, whom I came to trust. With their guidance, still living with my grandparents, I tried hard to stay out of trouble, prepared to go to school in the fall, and mowed lawns and did gardening to make money. I bought clothes and started looking and feeling better than ever, and pretty darn cute—all five feet of me with my brown ponytail, miniskirts, and still hard-to-repress sassy attitude.

Most important, I was no longer using substances to get by.

Things Fall Apart

It was a tenuous time for me. Sobriety and stability were still new. Then I fell "in like." The infatuation happened at an end-of-summer dance when I was still fifteen. I met a boy named Arnie and from the moment we first danced, he decided I was "the one" for him. I was delighted to be someone's dream girl, and so Arnie became my boyfriend. We kept a low profile and took our courtship slow, enjoying the process of getting to know each other. Unfortunately, a cousin of mine told Mom and Pop about it. They became terribly upset—not so much over the fact that I had a boyfriend, but that this boy was Mexican.

On the day they found out, my grandparents let me know in no uncertain terms that I could no longer have Arnie as a friend. In fact, soon after I went to bed that night, they came into my room and made it clear that I was forbidden to ever see him again. If I defied them on this, they warned me, I would go back into foster care. Not just me, they said, but my brother, too! Despite the late hour, I ran out of their house.

I felt crushed. The only place I could think of going was to the church. When I got there, the building was dark, but I was operating in survival mode, so I sneaked into the chapel. There, in the sanctuary, I stomped and yelled about the injustice of it all. Then I fell to the floor and cried my eyes out. I cried about Arnie, and everything else in my life that was missing—all the ordinary things a fifteen-year-old wants that I'd never had, like love, safety, and someone to believe in me.

I told the Lord that this was just not right. After all, I had turned my life around and handed it over to Him, and yet more terrible things were happening to me. If I continued seeing Arnie,

I would hurt my brother and get us both kicked out—and, most likely, separated again. Apparently, I screamed, cussed, and cried loud enough to get the attention of the church secretary who was working down the hall, and she notified the youth group leader, Ann, at her home.

Ann came walking through the sanctuary door with a worried expression on her face.

"What's wrong, Cindy?" she asked.

My first response was "Nothing!"

After Ann did some coaxing, I let her in a little, saying, "It's no use. Here I am cleaned up, going to school, working hard, and they take away the one thing I want: the one person who really cares about me. It's not fair. Aren't we supposed to love everyone?"

Ann kept her hand on my shoulder and just let me cry. When I finally ran out of tears and looked up, she said, "You can't see it now, Cindy. But God works in mysterious ways. Try to have some faith. All these troubles you see around you now just may help things turn out for the better—in the long run."

"Yeah, all you Christians say things like that," I said. "They don't mean anything!"

I wanted to believe Ann. But it was hard. She told me I'd have to accept her statement on faith. Little did I know how right she was, how much my life would turn around—for the better and from that point on.

Two weeks later, Ann and Dwight were given an emergency foster-care license, which permitted them to bring Jess and me into their home and hearts. I was so amazed that they trusted us enough to allow us into their home with their two young daughters. At fifteen years old, I had finally been placed with a family that could help me heal the wounds of my past and find new ways to feel and think.

When you're not given any reason to trust, you don't. The

bottom line was that up until this point in my life I knew I had to fend for myself—even if I did so in all the wrong ways. Oddly, even as the youngest of three children, early on I knew I possessed a reservoir of inner strength that I had to call on to protect myself or my siblings. Like a flower blossoming in the desert, with the unconditional love offered by Dwight and Ann, this inner strength of mine eventually did re-emerge and in healthier, less defensive (limbic-driven) ways. In fact, the same leadership potential that I'd once used with my girlie-girl gang would bring me to the work I'm doing in workshops around the world and sharing with you in this book.

A Young Brain Shaped by a Fear of Pain

When we're afraid, the limbic brain drives us to seek the short-lived comfort of impulsive behaviors—for present purposes, let's call them "the old ways." One common impulsive action that many of us learned at a very young age was abusing substances to avoid feeling more pain. Over time, these impulsive, self-medicating actions led us to addiction.

As anyone in recovery is aware, the behaviors stemming from addiction include neglecting our responsibilities and dumping uncontrolled negative feelings onto those we love and ourselves, ruining many relationships in the process. These are the results of a brain operating on autopilot with the limbic system in control.

My personal story offers multiple pictures of the limbic brain in action: my father's drinking to stave off the pain of abandonment; my mother's running away to pursue a dream at the expense of her husband and children and, ultimately, to the detriment of her own mental health. Of course, my teenage tough girl persona came straight out of my limbic brain. Each of these defensive personas and the actions they produced were driven primarily by a deep-seated fear—of being alone, of never being considered "special," of being hungry or hurt—among many others.

Our actions were futile attempts to avoid—or take flight from—the conflict, hurt, disappointment, or other difficult emotions our lifestyles and poor choices had generated. In these behaviors, we were acting on our limbic brains.

Do You Want Off the Treadmill?

What if there were a way to get out of this cycle of fear and reaction? What if you could defuse your fear and settle a conflict at home or work without entering the endless loop that has never gotten you anywhere beyond a short-term reward? What if a new behavior could lead you to meet your deeper unmet need? Would you take it? At this point, I suspect your answer is closer to "maybe" than "yes."

You're no doubt thinking, at least a little bit, that this other way of dealing with conflict is not reliable and as such may leave you vulnerable to all those people out there whom you *know*, in your heart of hearts, are out to get you.

Without using the language of science, my last foster parents, Ann and Dwight, introduced me to a life no longer ruled by fight or flight. It was they who first showed me that by trusting myself, and responding differently to people and things, my everyday life could be less difficult—and far more rewarding. Their greatest lesson, the one I return to throughout this book, is this: When thought comes before action, we no longer have to live in reaction and fear. However, before we can appreciate and apply those more positive ideas, we must understand the past—both our personal past and that of our human species, for they are one and the same.

A Brief Lesson in Neuroscience

GOODBYE LIMBIC, HELLO THINKING BRAIN

This chapter is about the brain. It's also about behavior, because words and actions are the primary manifestations of what goes on in our brains. That's why psychology is called a "behavioral science." In order to shift our primary behavior style from one that is largely instinctual and ruled by the limbic to another, more deliberate and thoughtful style of behavior dominated by the cortex, we must take a closer look at both human behavior and the brain systems behind it.

Leading from our limbic is a survival technique that many of us learned in our families or from time spent in unhealthy relationships later in life. If we learned to approach all conflict with the mind-set of fight or flight, we may be fleeing something that we actually need to remain involved with—for both practical and emotional reasons—like a hurt from the past or an imagined situation, like a partner's cheating.

Alternatively, if we have a history of responding reactively in relationships, it may be that, after a time, those relationships leave us, with the other person no longer wanting to live at the mercy of the uncertain reactions emanating from our limbic brains. Such a limbic-driven survival mentality teaches us to think the worst of others, and as we do, we can create a "self-fulfilling prophecy." In other words, because we expect awful behaviors from another person, our words and actions trigger exactly that in the other person, producing an ongoing cycle of miscommunication and mutual hurt.

To help us see these dynamics in our lives, I've created a set of composite men and women—characters drawn from thousands of real people I've counseled and trained. I've put them in typical situations where these common survival mentality habits are on display. I'm guessing much of what these characters experience will sound and feel very familiar to each of you.

Vignette 1. The long-term marriage of Bill and Sara is regaining stability after five years of estrangement and distrust caused by Bill's excessive drinking and an affair he had with a coworker, which came to light six months ago. Bill is now sober, and he and Sara are seeing a counselor to repair the damage done to their relationship.

They argue less often and their communication seems to be improving; that is, until today. While driving home from work, Sara spots Bill standing on the sidewalk in front of a hotel. She's about to pull over and say hello when she sees that his companion is a young, attractive woman and the two of them are having an animated conversation. Sara immediately puts two and two together and assumes Bill is having an affair, and possibly is drinking again. She goes home and spends the evening stewing about her suspicions. By the time Bill gets home from his regular AA meeting—a half hour later than usual—and offers Sara a warm greeting, she's furious and turns away from his kiss. In a tense exchange, Sara reveals her suspicions. Angry that his wife won't accept that the woman was a potential client he was escorting to a cab, Bill loses his temper and declares, on his way out the door, that he may as well get drunk if Sara is going to assume the worst of him anyway.

Vignette 2. Dan is a middle manager with just three years on the job at a manufacturing company that has seen its business fall off during the recent recession. Rumors have begun to fly about potential layoffs, but nothing concrete has come from upper management except directives for cost cutting and a hiring freeze. Without seniority, Dan assumes he'll be the first to go, if and when the pink slips start. He worries so much about it that his usual focus is gone. His reports are late, and he doesn't speak up at staff meetings for fear of saying the wrong thing and drawing negative attention to himself. His boss, Sally, has started to wonder what's going on with Dan, but she decides not to press the issue, wary that Dan's work performance will only deteriorate further if she criticizes him.

In these interactions, each person is reacting to a threat by using a fight-or-flight response. Sara vents her fury at Bill before even asking questions. Bill vows to get retribution for Sara's unfair accusations by drinking. Dan is ready to fly from his job without any concrete evidence that he's a target of rumored layoffs. Dan's boss, Sally, avoids what she fears would be a messy encounter by pretending not to notice Dan's performance change. Ironically, by using these limbic-driven behaviors, each contributes to creating the very outcome he or she fears the most.

Like the composite characters of Sara, Bill, Dan, and Sally in these vignettes, most of us grew up in homes that capitalized on limbic behaviors of fight or flight. As children, we were largely helpless onlookers to our parents' limbic-driven conflicts with each other. These early life situations then created emotional memories, behavior patterns, and corresponding neural pathways that shape how we respond to relationship conflict in our lives today.

When we're afraid (or tired, overwhelmed, sad, or any other extreme emotional state), the limbic brain drives us to seek the short-lived comfort of the old ways, habits like abusing substances in order to numb real or imagined pain. As stated earlier in this book, the behaviors that stem from addiction are the results of a brain operating on autopilot, with the limbic system in control.

Your brain basically controls your experience of the world—from movement to thinking, eating and sleeping, smells, sight, behavior—as well as your recent and remote memory and how you deal with those memories. The brain and your use of it determine whether you live an instinctual or determined-by-you life.

To help you visualize the inside of your brain, take your right index finger and place it on the top center of your head, and then take your left index finger and place it just above your ear in the middle of the skull. The limbic system is in the center of your cranium, exactly where your extended fingers would meet if they could enter your head. The limbic is the oldest system in your brain. Four hundred thousand (or so) years ago, when Homo sapiens first evolved on the savannahs of Africa, it was the largest part of the brain cavity; in fact, it took up most of the available space. The brain's main function in those "cave person" days (the first development of man/woman) was the instinct of fight or flight. This is the impulse that made man leap into action when a tiger came toward him. It would guide him to either take flight (run like heck the other direction) or fight ("I'm so hungry I'm going to kill this beast for dinner"). So, the primary purpose of our limbic brains was to react to our environment—a harsh one to be sure.

"Mammalian" You

The limbic system is named after the Latin word *limbus,* meaning "edge." It is also called the "old mammalian system" or the "mammalian brain." This is from the triune brain model, which splits the brain into three parts according to their location and functions. The other parts are the reptilian brain (or the brain stem) and the cerebral cortex (or the neocortex). These are responsible for "lower" and "higher" behavior, respectively. We will come back to the cortex later in this chapter.

Figure 1. Parts of the Brain

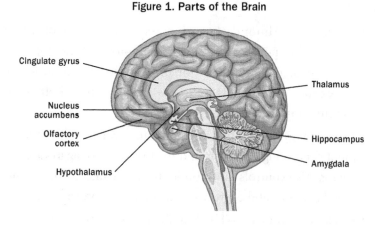

Besides the primary fight-or-flight responses, the limbic system is also the center of emotions, the regulation of memories, motivation, the interaction between emotional states and memories of physical stimuli, and physiological autonomic regulators, as well as hormones, sexual arousal, circadian rhythms, and some decision systems.

Although you may wonder if it's really necessary to learn how the limbic system functions, I recommend that you go a little further. Think of it like learning the mechanics of your car. You want to know where the alternator is located versus the starter or battery—especially if the car breaks down and there's a chance you might be able to fix the problem yourself. Similarly, if we are going to gain control over our impulses, it helps to be able to visualize how and where they happen.

The limbic system includes several structures in the cerebral pre-cortex and sub-cortex of the brain. Each plays an important role in making things run smoothly in the brain. Similar brain structures can be found in almost all warm-blooded creatures, such as dogs, cats, and mice. Reptiles do not have a similar brain structure; they possess only a brain stem.

The following structures are considered to be part of the limbic system:

- **Amygdala**—Almond-shaped mass of nuclei involved in emotional responses, hormonal secretions, and memory. Involved in signaling motivationally significant stimuli to the cortex such as those related to reward and fear and other social functions such as mating.

- **Cingulate gyrus**—A fold in the brain involved with sensory input concerning emotions and the regulation of aggressive behavior. Also controls autonomic functions such as heart rate, blood pressure, and cognitive and attentional processing.

- **Nucleus accumbens**—The brain's famed "pleasure center."

- **Hippocampus**—A tiny nub that acts as a memory indexer—sending memories out to the appropriate part of the cerebral hemisphere for long-term storage and retrieving them when necessary. Required for the formation of long-term memories and implicated in maintenance of cognitive maps for navigation.

- **Hypothalamus**—This structure, which is about the size of a pearl, directs a multitude of important functions. It wakes you up in the morning and gets the adrenaline flowing. The hypothalamus is also an important emotional center, controlling the signals that make you feel exhilarated, angry, or unhappy. It regulates the autonomic nervous system via hormone production and release. It affects and regulates blood pressure, heart rate, hunger, thirst, sexual arousal, and the sleep/wake cycle.

- **Thalamus**—A large, dual-lobed mass of gray matter cells that relay sensory signals to and from the spinal cord and the cerebrum cortex. It is the relay station between the two areas of the brain.

- **Olfactory cortex**—Receives sensory information from the olfactory bulb and is involved in the identification of odors.

In summary, the limbic system is responsible for controlling various functions in the body, like interpreting emotional responses, storing memories, and regulating hormones. The limbic system is also involved with sensory perceptions, motor function, and olfaction (sense of smell).

One way to better understand the limbic system is to familiarize yourself with some of its favorite phrases. These are the words we speak in self-defense, and to strike out at another person who we fear may threaten us in some way. Read them aloud (see sidebar) and check out how your body is feeling. A little more stressed than you were a moment ago?

**Words and Phrases We Often Use in
"Limbic Brain" Responses**

- How could you?
- You always . . .
- But!
- You never . . .

- You should . . .
- No!
- Absolutely not!

Often said with a finger pointing in the air or at someone—like you!

The Limbic System and Addiction

The limbic system is what engages when people become addicted. This is where the behaviors and habits of addiction are developed and stored, specifically, inside the nucleus accumbens. To figure out how the limbic system performs this magic, research was carried out with rats. The goal of researchers was to pin down the roles played by the nucleus accumbens and the neurotransmitter it releases—dopamine. Before we go any further, it's worth pointing out that every type of reward—food, sex, simple touch, laughter—increases the level of dopamine transmission in the brain. And so do a variety of highly addictive drugs, including stimulants such as cocaine and methamphetamine, by acting directly on the limbic system, which releases the dopamine.

In the rat experiments, the rats' brains were connected to electrodes that electrically stimulated their nucleus accumbens when they pressed a switch. The researchers found that the rats continued to press that switch no matter what else they were offered. Their newfound need for the dopamine came at the exclusion of everything else that had formerly brought them rewards, including sex and food. And lest you comfort yourself with the fact that you're not a rat, remember that rats and humans share 99 percent of the same genes.

To understand addiction is to understand that it is tied to our most primitive instinctual responses, which are controlled by the limbic system. As discussed, when we're afraid, the limbic brain drives us to seek the short-lived comfort of abusing substances to numb our terror, fear, or pain. No wonder relapse is so commonplace! Simply put, the limbic brain must be reined in through a series of cognitive trainings. The word *cognitive* refers to thinking; the essence of *Rein In Your Brain* is learning how to think your way through the fight-or-flight response to a frontal cortex response that is thoughtful and uses the concepts in this book. If you do, you will obtain a much firmer foundation for your continuing recovery and a happier, healthier lifestyle that you can pass along to others, including your children and family members.

Getting to Know Your Thinking Brain

Recent neuroscience suggests that we have access to a different, more positive, and more effective set of options than those driven by fear. We can use a different part of our brains—known as the cortex—to make more thoughtful choices about what we say and how we behave toward those around us. The limbic-driven, instinctual responses that most of us learned as children tend to make us over-react to conflict and not use the later-arriving "thinking part" of our brains known as the cortex. This front and center brain area is more suited to handling the kind of conflict that doesn't show up as a prehistoric beast or a warrior with spear in hand.

On top of the limbic brain system sits the cerebral cortex, or "thinking brain," with the thalamus acting as a liaison between the two. As this "top down" brain structure suggests, the purpose of the cortex is to apply the rationality we are all capable of to the in-stinctual responses that come out of our limbic system. The cortex gives us the ability to reason and think before we move a muscle or speak a word. As such, it is the most evolutionarily advanced part of us.

Unfortunately, few of us use the cortex when we face conflict or feel fear. Instead we go with our limbic-driven gut reaction. And that means our responses to adult problems are patterned on the ways we learned to respond to fearful situations as children.

If you come from a particularly chaotic, conflict-filled family of origin—such as mine, and millions of others—your limbic sys-tem tends to be much more developed than your cortex as a first line of defense against conflict. This part-instinct/part-learned legacy is our baggage. But that doesn't mean this state of being has to remain our future.

**Words and Phrases We Often Use in Cortex Responses—
the "Thinking Brain"**

- I believe . . .
- I wonder . . .
- Let's discover . . .
- Consider another idea . . .
- Let's back up the train.
- I would like . . .
- Often these things . . . thoughts . . . occur.
- Is it possible?
- Your thoughts . . . ideas . . . plans . . .
- Could it be . . . ?
- Yes, and . . .
- Have you thought . . . felt . . . believed . . . wondered . . . ?

Just as certain words and phrases reveal when the limbic part of our brains is in control, others indicate a more thoughtful approach to relating—especially in moments of conflict. As you say the phrases in the sidebar aloud, notice the difference in your mind and body compared to when you spoke aloud words and phrases favored by the limbic brain. Do you feel less stressed and more at ease?

With awareness and practice, using the thinking part of our brains will feel increasingly more "natural." Now let's begin with the first of my Ten Big Ideas adopted from addiction recovery and developed with the help of my colleague Chuck DeVore.

BIG IDEA 1

Stand Still in the Moment

Big Idea 1, Stand Still in the Moment, is your first line of defense against limbic reactions taking over a situation or relationship where you and another person are in conflict. This Big Idea is fundamental and foundational to reining in your impulses. The concept presented in this chapter can be applied to any relationship, personal or professional. Standing still in the moment may seem like a fairly simple task—until you're feeling tired, fearful, or hungry, or in any way overwhelmed by extreme emotion.

Let's look at a common situation that many parents encounter. It's the end of a long, trying day at work, and you're on your way to pick up your child from school. Traffic is bumper to bumper, and you're already fifteen minutes late. Finally, you arrive at the school. And as soon as you see your child's face, her frown reveals that she has had her own difficult day.

The two of you make it to the car, and as soon as you get her strapped into the car seat and you're sitting behind the wheel, she uses a whining voice to make the request that you are already dreading.

"Mom, can we go to McDonald's for dinner?"

You cringe. Driving through thick traffic for fast food is the last thing you want to do right now. Besides, money is tight until your next paycheck arrives. However, rather than try to scale down the sky-high tension building in the car, you opt to say nothing as you head in the direction of home.

Your daughter is not giving up. "Please, please, please can I have a Happy Meal?"

After the third time in as many minutes she repeats this request, you lose your temper. Speaking much too loudly, you say, "Just shut up!"

Is that the end of it? No, of course not.

"You never get me what I want," your child now wails.

"We just went to McDonald's the other day," you point out logically, and then add, "do you think money grows on trees?" As soon as you say it, you hate yourself for spouting the same silly question that your mother used to keep you from asking for things.

"You're so mean!" your daughter now says.

You clutch at the steering wheel and nearly drive through a red light.

What's really happening here?

Both of you are feeling under attack from the other. You both crave nurturing.

Whereas a soothing parental touch or a simple acknowledgment of her distress ("I know you're hungry and tired, Honey, and I'll fix you something you like as soon as we get home.") might reassure and calm your child, your voiced irritation only causes her to feel unloved—making a tough situation worse.

In this scenario, you both find yourselves in a "meeting of the limbic." The part of the brain where extreme emotions and impulsive reactions reside has become activated and irritated, leaving each of you in need of soothing. But comfort is the least likely thing either of you will receive in such a situation. Defenses are in full gear. Any new conversation you might attempt is already contaminated by the earlier exchange. Once you reach home, neither of you will leave the car feeling nurtured or loved. Certainly, neither of you will have a feeling of unconditional love for the other.

When this defensive dynamic starts early in a child's life, a deep neuropathway is created in her limbic brain to mirror this negative pattern of thought and behavior. The presence of such a well-established groove makes her far more likely to respond in exactly the same manner when the next conflict occurs—the next day or twenty years later! More immediately, the connection between parent and child begins to weaken as this cycle of mutual hurt and misunderstanding is established.

It is highly likely that you learned a similar limbic style of conflict from your parents, since it is often passed from one generation to the next. Memories of these interactions are stored, along with the neural pathways that reproduce the same behaviors. How

> **The first question to ask yourself as you *stand still in the moment*:**
>
> Are my behavior (gestures, tone, loudness of voice) and choice of words (negative, hurtful, name calling) going to
>
> 1. build the relationship up?
> 2. keep the relationship level?
> 3. tear the relationship down?

many of us have said, "Oh no, I told myself I would never act or sound like my parent! Here I go again, doing just that!" We often can't help repeating this limbic behavior since it has become so ingrained in us that it feels "instinctual."

If we wish to alter the way we deal with the people we love, and those we spend our days working alongside, we must *stand still* in moments of limbic irritation and check the tone and substance of what we are about to say or do in relation to the other person (see sidebar).

Your Brain Is Made of Jell-O

Not really, of course. But for a moment, think about your brain as if it were a bowl of Jell-O—in other words, highly malleable. Your brain creates pathways from repetition, like poking your finger into the gelatin. The more you do it, the deeper and wider the hole becomes. The scientific word for the result is a neuropathway. If I want to learn a new way of doing, saying, or being, I start at the top of that Jell-O brain and create a new neuropathway that gets deeper with repetition.

The creation of a new neuropathway to replace our old limbic-based style of conflict takes a lot of practice and repetition as well. When a familiar situation occurs, especially a conflict with a loved one or a coworker, the limbic brain automatically steers us into that older, deeper groove.

One way to ease the transition from an old groove to a new one is to simply *stop in the moment.* Once you stop, you can use conscious intention to redirect your brain. Taking a few moments to prevent yourself from speaking any further hurtful words or taking any more potentially negative actions literally stops your brain in its tracks. Inside the brain, you can picture chemical neurotransmitters that normally travel in one sequence shifting direction and taking a new, different-than-usual pathway.

This momentary stopping allows you to think through the possible consequences your words and actions may bring. *Will they build the relationship up, keep it level, or tear it down?* Pausing before speaking or acting, standing still in the moment, is more likely to result in a positive outcome.

Thinking Ahead

This different style of action and reaction can be practiced or rehearsed before you encounter the other person. If you suspect the situation ahead of you has the potential for conflict, you can consider the feelings you and the other person may already be experiencing. Before you pick up your child or go through the front door to greet a spouse, consider that they may have had their own tough day, a day with many stressful transitions in it. Think, or speak aloud, the following: "We're not going into that old familiar groove. We're moving over to the new pathway I've worked so hard to create."

Engaging your brain in this process of sensitivity, looking at the situation through the other person's eyes, will make a difference in how you approach the person in those all-important, tone-setting first seconds and minutes you are together.

This means thinking about how someone's entire day may have gone, from getting up in the morning to going to school or work. It means taking into account the variety of issues that may have risen in their day. It also means considering whether they have met (or may still need to meet) their basic needs for rest, food, and nurturing; perhaps they need to take time for a bit of solitude or exercise at the end of a day.

As human beings, we need to be held gently, spoken to with care, loved and adored. This is a tall order if we try to do it all at once. It is not so daunting when we think about and deliver these deliberate actions and words in small doses, and on a regular basis.

Does This Sensitivity Make Me a Weaker Person?

Standing still in the moment means letting go of the overly dominant "me" inside us in order to consider the highest good of the other person. We can also use this time to recognize our own needs. This two-step process—thinking about the needs of the other and oneself—is not done in a weak or self-effacing manner. To the contrary, it simply and powerfully allows you to take a stance that communicates that we all need to be heard and felt in a way that shows regard for each other.

If taking this stance feels difficult to us, it's only because our limbic brains have run the show for so long. However, there is much to gain from making this shift. If I can slow my brain down to engage with the other person, I can add to her feeling of being loved and cared for. If I stand still in the moment, if I look into the other person's eyes (that means getting down to a child's eye level) and communicate in a positive way, I will be enabling his brain to be in sync with mine—in a more open, less defensive emotional embrace.

Being on the giving or receiving end of positive interaction teaches the brain to move away from the limbic. Then we don't tend to follow the impulse to defend ourselves, since we are taking control of our brains and deliberately thinking through how we want to affect the other person. Instead of "winning an argument," we reach for mutual benefits. This moves us from the reactive limbic self to a more "proactive," cortex-based way of thinking and being.

When you delay your reaction to a provocative situation or comment, you intentionally place yourself in a state of suspension, signaling to your neurotransmitters that they need to come up with a better path forward. Suspension, or standing still in the moment to consider your deliberate response, gives you more—not less—power in the situation. You are no longer "dragged along" by your limbic brain!

Standing still and thinking about the impact of your next words and actions also creates an opportunity for mutual solution-focused problem solving. By having a conversation with the other person regarding how the day went, you consider whether one or both of you are feeling out of sorts, and what would help the two of you enter into and enjoy your "shared time" together. Here's some really good news: When our limbic feels loved and adored, it does not look to other substances and behaviors (drugs, alcohol, food, sex, or any type of excessive emotional pleasure) to be fed.

Remembering that limbic reactions are learned early in life

through our family systems, it's important to understand the dynamics and styles of communication and conflict that ruled those family interactions. The next section introduces five family styles of communication in conflict.

What's Your Conflict Style?

Although most conflicts we face in our relationships are driven by fear-based, defensive words and actions, the very same limbic feelings and thoughts can manifest quite differently in different people. To demonstrate these differences, I use the Thomas-Kilmann Conflict Mode Instrument (available at http://www.kilmanndiagnostics .com/catalog/thomas-kilmann-conflict-mode-instrument). Its purpose is to help us identify our individual styles of communicating when we experience conflict with another person or persons. This tool is used therapeutically by addiction counselors and other professionals, and increasingly, by employers to help individuals and teams resolve work-based conflicts. I have frequently used it with positive results when counseling clients and their families. Knowing how we and the other party behave in a conflict can be a great resource when we try to step back from those behaviors. As we stand still in the moment, each of us can use this knowledge to take another path forward.

How to Use the Family Styles of Conflict Tool

Typically, several styles of communication operate within a family in conflict. In fact, the same person may use more than one style in a situation or a different style in different situations. Fortunately, these styles are distinct enough that they are easy to self-identify— once we understand their primary motivations, attitudes, and behaviors.

When I use this tool in counseling, I usually ask clients to answer the questions twice. The first time I instruct them to respond as if they were in a work situation, and then, the second time, in personal relationships or home situations. Sometimes the results are different and sometimes not. It seems we are more careful at work in our responses than we are at home. It also seems that our concerns about keeping a job may overrule our need to keep a relationship, or we believe that our families will put up with more from us than our employer will.

In many cases, we may be terribly mistaken, so it is critical that we keep in mind how important all relationships are and do our best to understand our responses, where we learned them, how hurtful they can be, and how we can change them to be more healthy.

Please review and determine which of the following five styles you use most frequently when experiencing conflict.

Keep in mind that these styles do not come out as much when we're feeling positive and warm in relationship to others. However, they are very present when we're at odds with another person or persons. After reviewing the five styles, create your family circle of conflict communication styles, aka your "Family Pie Chart" (see pages 35–37).

Style 1: The Competer

This style carries an attitude of "I'm going to win and you are going to lose." The Competer believes that winning or losing are the only two possible outcomes of any conflict. As such, losing is associated with incompetence, a lack of status, and weakness. Winning is associated with status, power, and competence. To the Competer, winning is of prime importance, even to the point of hurting others. The Competer believes that we live in a dog-eat-dog world, where nice guys/gals finish last. Competers value their own personal goals and wants above all else. This means that, for them, relationships can become disposable. The method the Competer uses to control others is through the expression of resentment and anger. People respond out of fear to this person and may be controlled by that fear.

Style 2: The Avoider
This style carries the attitude of "fighting is useless, hopeless, and punishing." The Avoider believes that conflict results in both persons losing more than they gain, so instead of staying in a fight, the Avoider opts for flight. The leaving can be physical or mental, or it can be done with the aid of an object (book, video game, TV) or a substance of choice. The Avoider does not want to lose control. For the Avoider, getting angry causes a loss of control. Further, losing control is unfair, so this person believes it is better to leave. The Avoider may also adopt the role of a detached observer, viewing the conflict with no personal investment or looking to discover what is causing it. Avoiders roll with the situation and are ready for the next day—of course, without resolving the original issues that resulted in their avoiding behavior. Avoiders don't value their own stake or that of the other person in the conflict, leaving both parties in a quandary of not knowing where to turn next for help. The method the Avoider uses to control others is by withdrawing. Other people in relationship with an Avoider are not able to get a real gauge on what the Avoider may think or feel about the conflict at hand. The Avoider often withdraws from the relationship by removing other tangible supports to a partner's well-being, such as money or sex.

Style 3: The Accommodator
This style carries the attitude that relationships are fragile and that they cannot endure any difficulty, or differences of opinion. Therefore, Accommodators feel they must give up their own personal needs and goals to keep peace in the relationship. Often, the Accommodator fears losing the relationship, and therefore appeases the other person by ignoring or denying problematic

behavior. Accommodators value their relationships more than themselves and therefore lend themselves to being ruled by the other person. They also hold in their feelings, and act like everything is fine—that is, until the pressure gets so heavy, they blow up. I call this the "Mt. St. Helens effect" being played out . . . tick, tick, tick, BOOM! This is the case when a seemingly "nice" person suddenly explodes, doing something "out of character." The way Accommodators control others is by guilt. After all, in their minds, they have done *so much* to support the relationship.

Style 4: The Compromiser
This style carries an attitude that relationships ought to be fair, so each person *should* get a fair share from a conflict. The Compromiser thinks it's only right that each party get something out of the dispute, even if they both lose a little. This is a variation on win/lose, only the losses are limited. It sounds good. The trouble is that one of the two parties has to play the judge, determining what is fair. Often the question of whose rules are being applied becomes another issue of contention. I call this a "rules-based" solution to conflict. In a sense, no one really wins or loses here. Compromise may appear to be a healthy style of conflict, when in fact it doesn't take into consideration the whole situation or the needs of the parties involved. The way the Compromiser controls is by the use of special rules.

Style 5: The Collaborator
The Collaborator is the ideal conflict style. It carries an attitude of "win-win," meaning both parties can come out as winners. This style of thinking through conflict uses behaviors that are different from those used in the other four styles. Importance and value are attached to both parties, and to the relationship. The goals for each person are not seen as mutually exclusive. The Collaborator recognizes that conflict is bound to happen because we are differ-

ent people with our own fabric of life. The Collaborator believes that most differences come from an incomplete understanding. There is also a personal sense of tolerance and acceptance of differences, and that each person has the right to his or her feelings in this conflict. It is how the conflict is dealt with that is important to the Collaborator. The precise way forward through a conflict is to first differentiate between the feelings each party has. Then the parties must know how the fabric of each person's life (meaning their background) affects this situation—the relationship between each person's real needs and the conflict at hand. The issue is then solved by integrating these concepts. The aim of the Collaborator is not to control; it is to understand the other person's perceptions. This creates more closeness between the parties by taking into consideration the feelings, points of view, and fabric of their respective lives. Real power is seen in the mutual relationship, and the highest value is seen if both parties are being honored by the problem solving/solution focus. Mutual understanding, mutual respect, mutual regard for both sides' winning, and mutual joy are included in the outcome!

Exercise: Filling in Your Pie Chart

Most of us were not raised in families that used the collaborative style as a basis for conflict resolution. We were raised in families where the other four styles were more often used—styles most likely passed down from one generation to the next.

Take a moment now and think about each family member's behaviors in times of conflict. How did the father figure in your family most often react in conflict? And what about the mother figure? Then consider you and your siblings. How did each of you tend to react when there was lots of yelling or stony silences going on between your parents? Were there other persons in the household, and how did they affect you in times of conflict?

Some other useful questions to consider:

- Who talked out their anger?
- Who hid it or avoided it?
- Who exploded and pushed their anger onto others?
- Was there a person who tried to be the peacemaker? How did the person do this?
- How did family members react to each other's style?
- Who held control in the family and was it ever questioned?
- How was conflict resolved in the family?
- When did you know that the argument, flight, or conflict was over?

To assist you in thinking through these questions, first make a list of your family members, writing down their name and role (i.e., Doris/wife/mother, Jess/husband/father, Kathy/daughter/ sister, Jess/son/brother, Cynthia/daughter/sister). Then consider how each person initially reacted to conflict in the household. Try to think of specific situations or issues. For example, typical situations involve disagreements about money and parenting decisions. Perhaps you were the catalyst for one or more such conflicts. Some of these may have been recurring situations, and they may be issues that still affect the family today.

As you list each member of the family, write down what you consider to be that person's primary style in conflict, as well as their secondary style. People tend to use their primary style until it fails, and then flip to a backup or secondary style. List the primary and secondary styles for each person in the family. In looking at each person, including yourself, you might consider whether there were several Competers in the family. If so, how did they react to each other?

Then, most importantly, consider how the dynamics of your

family styles may have affected how you react and respond in conflict in your life today.

Next, we'll try using a tool for recording these reflections—one that permits you to visualize these key family dynamics.

Family Conflict Styles

Creating a visual representation of your family conflict communication styles is useful for self-understanding, and it can be a handy reference to help make the most of subsequent exercises in this book. A simple pie chart, available in many word processing programs, can illustrate how communication styles in family conflict can differ and then interact with each other. To demonstrate, I've put my family of origin and our conflict communication styles into a pie chart format. As you view it, keep in mind the story of my childhood and teen years.

Figure 2. Cynthia's Family Styles

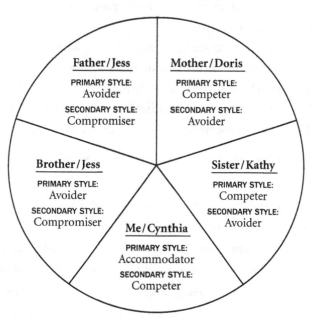

Father / Jess
PRIMARY STYLE:
Avoider
SECONDARY STYLE:
Compromiser

Mother / Doris
PRIMARY STYLE:
Competer
SECONDARY STYLE:
Avoider

Brother / Jess
PRIMARY STYLE:
Avoider
SECONDARY STYLE:
Compromiser

Sister / Kathy
PRIMARY STYLE:
Competer
SECONDARY STYLE:
Avoider

Me / Cynthia
PRIMARY STYLE:
Accommodator
SECONDARY STYLE:
Competer

Repeating Family Conflict Styles in Adulthood

As we grow from childhood to adulthood, we often re-create our family conflict styles in other relationships. Because we're familiar and comfortable in the roles we assumed in our original family, we have these styles embedded in our brains. We might also instinctually look to find relationships that will allow us to work out unresolved issues from our family of origin and "replay" unhealthy patterns, with the goal of getting it "right" or better.

In order to rein in your brain and live in thoughtful recovery, it is vital that you become aware of the communication style(s) you tend to use in conflicts, both your primary and secondary styles. This self-awareness allows you to regain your own sense of self and personal power. It also enables you to assess the styles you may have learned in your family that you no longer want in your life. You can then make a deliberate effort to change those behaviors and move to the collaborative style of communication and thereby reduce conflict and gain more power over your brain and the outcomes in your life.

Many of us feel we are Collaborators, yet when push comes to shove, we find one of the other four styles emerging. Few of us grew up in homes where conflict was dismantled in the collaborative style. Most of us came from families that were stuck in the generational behaviors of compete, avoid, compromise, or accommodate.

Six Steps You Can Take to Become More Collaborative

1. Make a vow that you are not going to react impulsively from your limbic brain when you next find yourself in a potential conflict situation.

2. Ahead of any conflict, develop a proactive plan in which you acknowledge your conflict communication style(s).

3. When a conflict arises, stop and linger in the moment; use this pause to look at which conflict communication style

each person is employing at that stage of the conflict; consider how the other person's style is affecting you and how your style is potentially affecting him or her.

4. Determine if your style is helping or hurting the relationship.

5. Agree to stop or back up the train to prevent it from running down that old track (of behavior) if you have already started down the "Limbic Trail."

6. Consider adopting a more collaborative style and look for the win-win for both of you.

Let's Go Back to Big Idea 1: Stand Still in the Moment

You've gained some insights about your own and other family members' conflict styles. You may see that you typically react by blaming or shaming (Competer), by walking away from the situation (Avoider), or by acquiescing to the situation and holding it inside of yourself (Accommodator).

Now think about an alternative style. Consider taking a more proactive approach by understanding the other person's perspective, conflict style, and emotional fabric and how these elements play into the conflict at hand; that is, try taking on the collaborative style.

By standing still in the moment or backing up the train when you begin to derail, you can try on new behaviors such as those suggested in the six steps above. By now, I hope, you have noticed that the old behaviors are taking you down that same old track, and you have decided that you don't want to go there anymore. This decision is a key step in reining in your brain and gaining a new perspective of where your life and relationships can move.

Lingering in moments of conflict and re-establishing communication based on the new style you want to achieve will help you drop the baggage of past relationships that went sour. Working to avoid treating others like the "enemy" or trying to win every argument allows the relationship room to expand into more intimate conversation. Letting go of the need to accommodate in order to sustain a relationship relieves both people of the guilt from past interactions. Put another way, your relationship no longer needs to pack its bags and go on another guilt trip!

Successful, happy, and healthy relationships require mutual awareness and responsiveness that is cortex based. Otherwise, you are living in the limbic, blaming the other person. Eventually, that relationship is going to explode or implode with neither party holding on to the core belief that it is worth preserving. This is where the idea of a disposable relationship comes in. If it doesn't work out, each party assumes they will just go get another partner, where the same dynamics ensue.

When you learn to apply Big Idea 1 to your relationships, by standing still in the moment and giving yourself and your partner time to back up the train, you create new pathways in your brain. The more you practice it, the more it becomes instinct. The more it becomes instinct, the more balanced and centered you become. There are myriad ways to remember to stop what you're doing and stand still in the moment. Here are three suggestions.

Repeat a Mantra

A mantra is a phrase that you can repeat aloud or in your mind. It slows down your brain and gives you control of your limbic. A repeated mantra helps the brain become more centered and less intense in the heat of the moment.

Your mantra could be to answer these three questions before you allow a discussion to escalate: "Will what I am about to say and the way I am going to say it build the relationship up? Will it keep things level? Will it tear the relationship down?"

There are many other mantras that can reassure you that

change is possible. "I think I can, I think I can" is a mantra from *The Little Engine That Could* that you may have read as a child. You can play around with other phrases and decide which mantra or mantras are meaningful to you and will best work for you and your brain to move from an instinctual mind-set to a deliberate new track.

Ask Yourself: What Is the Real Issue?

Another technique for standing still in the moment is to figure out what the real issue is in your immediate conflict. Sometimes what we think is the real issue is not the real issue at all. We may be fighting over going to a certain restaurant, when in fact the real fight is about a partner's credit card usage the past month.

The real argument is often shadowed by past relationship experiences. Until we are willing to look at where this feeling is coming from, we may not be able to recognize the real issue putting stress on the relationship. Is it a feeling from a past marriage or partnership? Is it from your family of origin? How do I figure this out? More often than not, it is the past hurts in our lives that stand in the way of sorting out what we are really feeling in the present.

Make a Chronogram of Your Emotional History

A chronogram is a diagram of our emotional history, particularly the hurt that often reoccurs in our lives. These emotions are embedded in our limbic and rise up when we're triggered by current situations. As a result, we create the same unhappy outcome over and over again.

See the sample chronogram on the next page, and create your own at the end of this chapter. Include feelings such as abandonment, loss (friends, family, things), anger, humiliation, loneliness, despair, rejection, and resentment. Write down each feeling as well as the age and circumstance when you first remember strongly

experiencing these feelings. Write down how that situation was resolved or not resolved. Are there similar issues or feelings happening in your life today? Do you carry over some of these feelings to
current relationships or circumstances without connecting them
to this earlier time? Do you look for them to "show up" again in
new relationships, even creating circumstances so that they play
themselves out (like a self-fulfilling prophecy) so you can feel jus-
tified in the outcome? We tend to re-create the issues that are unresolved in our lives. We try over and over to resolve them, often
without new tools or different ways of looking at the issue. We
become stuck in that feeling or circumstance.

Table 1. Sample Chronogram of Past Emotions

Age	Event	Feeling	Resulting Behaviors
6	Dog lost	Sad	Fear of loving someone
12	Parents divorced	Abandoned, Confused	Fear of commitment
14	School fight	Overwhelmed	Loss of self-esteem
20	Argument with friend	Frustrated	Not worth the energy to fight
24	Breakup with boyfriend	Betrayed	All men are trouble
30	Mother passed away	Sorrow, Depressed	Reinforces losses

It is important when learning to stand still in the moment that
we develop the capacity to resist moving back into the argument
or situation, to run away from it, or give in to it. It will prove much
more beneficial and healthy to work *with* rather than *against* the
energy the other person brings to the situation. Wait and learn
how to get into sync with the feelings and circumstances at work

in each conflict between you and another person. Stand still in the moment and know that there is a misunderstanding that needs to be sorted out. Remaining in a place of suspension during the time it takes for the initial reaction to be adjusted in your brain is the key to this very fundamental Big Idea. Decide what behavior you want to move to in order to resolve the conflict and not just instinctually respond from your limbic memory.

Standing Still in Your Pain before Moving Forward

I shared earlier that, in my life, I experienced physical, sexual, emotional, and nutritional abuses growing up. These abuses are deep in the emotions of my limbic system. They rage forward when a current situation brings up emotions from my past. At the age of four or five, my first sexual abuses began to take place in my grandparents' home by a family member. This family member was older than me by about eleven years. I looked up to this person, and yet when the sexual abuse started to happen, I knew something was wrong or off. I became confused with feelings of love for this family member, but also feelings of betrayal. I could not speak of it to the family, as there were already comments from the family and others that I had to be careful not to develop into my mother and be free with my sexuality the way she was.

The older family member who was abusing me sexually knew this, as he heard it over and over again and used that "against me" by telling me that if I said anything it would come back on me since I was causing it to happen. It became instilled in my brain to accommodate the situation and find ways to go to a different place in my mind when the sexual abuses happened.

Years later, after I married Arnie, there were times when

we would clash over sexual issues, and I would revert to my old behaviors instead of realizing he was a different person, this was a different situation, and we were not children. It took years of standing still in the moment of these feelings and sorting out what was real today and what was a carryover from my childhood. Learning to stand still in the pain, dissect it, and transform it by taking back my personal power was liberating to both myself and to our relationship. Learning to speak about it gave it less power over my mind. Sorting out the issues of mental illness and abuse that led to my family members' sick behaviors helped me to see that it was not my fault, and also gave me a context for their behaviors that helped me to understand how this could occur. Thinking it through gave my mind the freedom to release the negativity and anger, and gave way to feeling sad that this abuse occurred. Resolving the sadness of a loss of childhood safety and internalizing that to recover from the hurt, pain, and trauma moved my mind from reacting at a high level of emotional response to any given sexual situation in my adult sexual relationships to a more neutral or lower emotional response reaction that was more appropriate to that current specific situation. We all have internal trauma from which we need to recover and heal. What is important is how we put that pain and trauma in the understanding area, or cortex, of our brains in order to resolve what we can and release what is possible.

This is not done just once. It is peeling back pain, hurt, and trauma, layer by layer, until we reach the core. The core is the flash point for our feelings, and once we release the core through understanding and forgiving, our brains no longer hold it so tightly in the limbic.

Emotional Chronogram Exercise

A chronogram is a useful method for charting your feelings. Create a table like this one and identify points in your life when you recall conflict or anger intruding on your relationships. What was happening at the time? How did you feel?

Age	Event	Feeling	Resulting Behaviors

BIG IDEA 2

Do Not Assume Intent

When we're in pain, especially emotional pain, it is tempting to blame our misery on those with whom we maintain the closest relationships. There are several reasons for this. The people closest to us are typically those who cause us to feel most passionately. These are the significant others we are in love with. These are also the people with whom we have the most history. They are our romantic partners and spouses, children, close family members, and close friends. That history comes in all flavors. It may be positive, negative, or, at the very least, confusing. These are the people who are also closest to us physically, within "striking distance," and get the full force of our pain when we act it out.

To "not assume intent" means letting go of presumption. When we're engaged with another person in conflict, every painful and uncomfortable action or communication coming from that person feels like a premeditated attack on us. The discomfort or pain we are feeling is most likely not purposeful on the part of the other person. Most likely the person does not even realize the amount of pain or discomfort we are feeling. And yet, because we are emotionally intimate with that person, we assume he or she knows the pain we are in and all the reasons why we are experiencing those excruciating feelings. The majority of pain in long-term relationships is caused not by intentional acts but by misunderstandings and accidental collisions by two well-intentioned people.

Communicating in relationships is sometimes like conducting important business in a cubicle with ten people jammed into it. Sooner rather than later, people are going to step on each other's toes without the intention to do so! That's why we can never assume we know the other person's intent! When you feel hurt or slighted by another person's words or actions, ask that person: "By saying or doing [fill in the blank with what was said or done], did you mean for me to feel [hurt] [angry] [disappointed]?" Fill in your feeling.

In reining in our brains, we make an inner agreement, as a commitment to ourselves, that even if we think we know what the other person intended, we will check it out before we act on that assumption. In other words, we will not assume we know the other person's intent.

This means that when you find yourself offended by something someone says or does that you perceive as an attack, you are not going to "go there" without changing your approach and asking for (1) clarification or (2) more information by using direct questions.

This clarifies for you and the other person what was said and/ or done, how that led to your reaction, and whether this was what the other person had in mind. If it was that person's intent to cause a hurtful reaction, this will most likely be revealed in the communication. And then you will have put him or her on alert that, from here on, you will "call out" words or behaviors that are hurtful—not out of anger—because you want to communicate more effectively.

It is helpful to use Big Idea 1 (Stand Still in the Moment) and Big Idea 2 (Do Not Assume Intent) together. Slow down your limbic reactions and look for a deeper understanding of the other person's emotional fabric before you develop your thoughts and plan what you'll do or say as a result of that thinking. You can always develop a strategy of response once you know the reality of the other person's intentions. You might save yourself the embarrassment of reading the situation incorrectly and responding in a way that is harmful to the relationship. Knowing what you need in and from the relationship, and knowing what the other person needs, helps to build stronger communication lines. It also allows you both to move past the assorted relationship baggage we all carry.

Keeping your limbic still and allowing the other person time to clarify intentions will put the ball in his or her court to respond and will strengthen your personal integrity. Then, the two of you can move into mutual solution-focused problem solving, working as a team to build trust in the relationship.

You Said You Would Call Me!

When we feel hurt in a common situation, such as when someone promises to call and then doesn't, we might assume this lapse was intentional, rude, or disrespectful. In the very least it was insensitive. Due to this reaction, the next time we're in the presence of that person, we may act distant, cold, or uncaring. At this point, our limbic is irritated, with the natural instinct to blame, shame, and get even.

However, depending on your conflict communication style, the response to this perceived affront may be different. If I am a "blame-me" person (Accommodator), I may act as though I made the error. In this way, I am taking on more than my fair share of responsibility for the relationship. My willingness to work harder on my own "wonderfulness" will, in the end, cause the other person to feel bad for not holding up his end of the relationship. So, without directly confronting his intent, as an Accommodator I call into question his behavior by comparing it to my own admirable efforts. In this way, I am acting as if I am the "angel" in the relationship.

If I am a "blame-both" (Avoider) person, when I see the other person after the non-call, my response will be icy. I won't try to learn why she didn't call, and I'll act as if it does not matter to me. My attitude is that if she is going to be insensitive to me, I will just give the same back to her! A negative effect on me yields a negative effect on the other person and no one wins, certainly not the relationship.

If I am a "blame-you" (Competer) person, when I see the other person after the non-call, my response will be anger and blame. Again, I will not try to learn if there was something that caused him not to call; I'll assume that he purposefully did not call and wanted to hurt me. I might shout and blame and tell him how disrespectful or uncaring he is. My message: "How could you do this to me?" The trouble with this response is that I am only blaming, not searching for other possibilities.

The most difficult part of not assuming intent is learning not to lead with instinct. We all have a voice inside our heads that rises up to defend us when we experience pain or discomfort. It is up to *you* how you react to that instinctual (limbic) brain. This is especially true now that you know you have the option of training your brain to move from the limbic to the frontal cortex, where you can respond by using a more thoughtful approach, which is the fifth style of communication in conflict: the Collaborator.

So How Do I Discover Another Person's True Intent?

The next step is to learn how to seek the information from the other person in a manner that is not shameful or blameful. As illustrated in the "But-you-didn't-call!" example, if we lead from our limbic, blame is embedded in the process and the words we use to take in information and to ask for information. Danger resides in the loaded questions or responses we give.

Examples of limbic-driven, loaded questions:

- Why would you do such a stupid thing?
- What the heck is wrong with you? What the heck is going on with you?
- Did you mean to be [rude, mean, insensitive]?
- Don't you love me? Is this why you are so unaffectionate in public? What are you trying to hide and from whom?
- So what—is everything about you?

Examples of cortex-driven, information-seeking questions:

- I am confused as to what you said and what you meant. Will you please explain it to me?
- Will you help me remember what we agreed to the other day in regard to this issue?
- It seems that showing affection in public [or any other behaviors] is uncomfortable for you. Will you please tell me if this is so? Will you tell me why it is that way, and what causes this for you?
- It appears from your statement that you feel I did something to hurt you. Will you please tell me what that is so I can understand your perspective?
- When you said I did this all wrong, my reaction is that you didn't fully understand what I was doing. This caused me to think that you don't value my opinion or way of doing things. Is this what you meant? It would be helpful in the future if you'd share what you like about what I'm doing, what causes you concern, or what you think I can improve on. Does this work for you?

To help move from blame to solution-focused problem solving or understanding, it is important to ask the other person to participate with you in the process. Here are some suggestions for doing that:

- Describe the events leading up to the misunderstanding or confrontation.
- Give examples of what you thought you heard or saw, being careful not to blame or shame in the examples.
- Name the effect this misunderstanding or confrontation had on you (hurt, confusion, humiliation) and do not indicate that the other person purposefully intended to do this to you.
- Leave the door open for the other person to explain her or his perspective and intentions. This may take some time, and your ability to stand in the moment may need to be engaged.
- From the information given, begin to draw your conclusions and decide within that framework how you will respond—keeping in mind how that response will build up, keep level, or tear down the relationship.
- If the other person tells you that the behavior or communication was not intended to hurt, embarrass, or affect you in a negative manner, then believe him or her. Do this unless there is solid evidence otherwise.
- Ask whether the person would be willing to change that behavior if it is hurtful, confusing, or uncomfortable in order to avoid further pain in the relationship.

In Summary, When We Assume Intent:

- We jump to conclusions—often the incorrect conclusion.
- We wonder, "Is the other person trying to control me?"
- We are concerned that we will not be heard so we push for our way.

- We assume we understand the fabric of the other person in the situation, not really connecting with what that may be at the time.

- We can be quick to show anger and become resentful or vengeful with a revengeful "I'll-show-you" attitude.

- We can quickly cover for the other person in order to avoid learning more about his or her intention.

Why Are Relationships So Hard?

Let's start with a simple truth: Relationships are the hardest thing we will ever do. They are complicated and they never seem to follow the path we have in mind. They are confusing because we have premeditated concepts of what relationships "should" or "could" be like. We learn these notions as we are growing up, straight out of our favorite fairy tales. The most dominant, and in some ways dangerous, fantasy is that because we know he or she is out there somewhere waiting for us, we will eventually find that "perfect person"—our own prince or princess who will somehow be ready and willing to make us happy for life.

The difficulty with these dreamy expectations is that we don't leave them behind in childhood. Instead, no matter how old we get, or how contradictory our real-life experiences of relationships may be, we continue to believe in fairy tales. We grow up with wholly unrealistic expectations that our "love relationships" should be easier than any other relationships—simply because we are *in love!*

Misunderstandings commonly happen because we do not understand the *process of relationships.* What we do *not* learn growing up is that there are five stages in any relationship, which are both predictable and entirely natural. The intensity or length of time in each stage is dependent on the maturity levels, expectations, and life experiences of the persons involved. That is, they are "relationship dependent."

The Five Stages of Relationship

These five stages—Honeymoon, Disillusionment, Misery, Awakening, Peace and Calm—can apply to any close relationship in our lives. This includes a relationship with a lover, child, friend, or co-worker, and even with yourself. To discover how these stages apply to your life and your closest relationships, you'll need to take a trip back into your personal history. And, because our romantic love relationships provide the clearest window on how these stages develop and affect us, we'll focus there first.

Stage 1: Honeymoon

Your relationship with a current partner or significant other may have begun a while ago, or it may have started very recently. No matter how long ago, think back to what it was like for you in the very beginning, the special things you did with that person, the places you went, the special gifts you gave, the songs you shared, and, most importantly, the feelings you felt. What were those feelings? Let's explore them now.

The following are some examples of feelings common to the beginning of a new relationship:

- excitement
- uncertainty
- anticipation
- fear or anxiety
- hopefulness
- thoughtfulness
- carefulness
- a rush!

Think about some of the things you did to impress or put your best foot forward for the benefit of this significant other at the start of your relationship:

- cleaned up, dressed up, and showed up!
- took care not to burp or fart (at least in the beginning)
- wore your best undergarments (just in case)
- communicated—a lot!
- listened
- shared your dreams
- gave gifts: cards, letters, text messages, flowers, candy, things you made
- planned special dates at interesting places and did fun things
- spent time and money

The Honeymoon stage of a love relationship is typically seen as the most romantic time. It's a time for exploring and learning about each other. Right from the start, our endogenous endorphins (the natural opioids produced during exercise, excitement, pain, and orgasm) begin bathing our brain. These "feel-good" chemicals cause us to see that person as the most attractive, most interesting, most enjoyable-to-be-with person in the whole wide world and, of course, we want to be with the person! And only that person! We wear bedroom clothing that reflects the excitement of the relationship: cute and frilly nighties, fun and playful bed wear, or nothing at all!

Our brain keeps telling us that this is the "right person," and everything he or she says during this stage seems to fit our image of true love. In this stage, we are also so happy to have found the right person that we might miss any warning signs that he or she *may not be* the right one after all.

This is especially true for those of us who are attracted to "bad boys" or "bad girls," people who are exciting to be with, but who will eventually hurt us. Those of us who grew up in abusive homes or relationships have a tendency to be attracted to these types. We do not recognize in the beginning of a relationship that it fits a familiar negative pattern because our limbic system is giving us a natural high and producing a single-minded desire to be with that person. There may also be a familiarity we feel about this person, which, though unconscious, harkens back to family-of-origin dynamics now ingrained in our brains.

This chemical bath can last up to several years, slowly wearing down and offering glimmers of the real person behind the veil. It is often advised not to marry in the first two years of a relationship, especially if past choices in relationships have followed the same pattern. This delay allows for the chemicals in our brains to dissipate and give the frontal cortex time to engage, prompting us to look more rationally at the relationship and what it offers in the long term.

On the other hand, there would be fewer relationships (and fewer babies born) without the Honeymoon stage. It is undeniably fun, and for some people it is the only stage in which they feel comfortable or good. It's the reason people get together. It's part of our instinct to procreate. This is a built-in human mechanism to ensure that our race continues. Some relationships have long Honeymoons, and others are shorter. Yet, in many relationships, it is during the Honeymoon that babies are made. People who only want to feel the ecstasy of the Honeymoon stage will find themselves losing interest as their natural opioids run down. Such people typically end a relationship once it begins to move into the second stage—Disillusionment.

Since the Honeymoon stage brings the highest-producing level of endorphins, persons looking for this rush, whether in recovery from an addictive substance or not, may find that this stage is addictive by itself! They may not want to experience any other stage. These folks are called "Honeymoon Hoppers," as they break off and move to the next "Honeymoon" as soon as the endorphins wear off, often moving from relationship to relationship, never committing beyond the first stage. Later in life, these very same people are the ones who begin to regret that they did not "stick with" a relationship or the children it produced.

There is little maturity or real intimacy in this level of relationship. The brain is bathed in lust versus commitment. Commitment does not happen in the limbic—only the seemingly sweet sensations of the Honeymoon. It would be helpful if persons who prefer this stage were up front about what they desire, giving the other person a warning that a mature and long-term relationship is unlikely to develop. Unfortunately, most people don't—they may even be unaware of their relationship pattern, or they blame the other person when the Honeymoon's over. The Honeymoon stage is something we may want to pay attention to and use to make more thoughtful decisions in the future.

Stage 2: Disillusionment
Sorry to burst the bubble, but you knew this was coming. The second stage of relationships is referred to as the Disillusionment stage or Disillusionment. This stage is also referred to as the "familiarization" or "adjusting to reality" stage. At this point, the endorphins in your limbic brain are not producing at the same level, so the rush of the relationship has slowed down. This may also mean the level of communication, sex, and general carefulness between the two of you has shifted to a more relaxed phase. No longer are you consumed with the same desire to fill every available second with the other person.

In fact, at this stage, you may be seeing more of the other person's flaws. The things that attracted you are now "un-attracting" you. If you were attracted in the beginning to the love and attention the person showed for his or her family, now you wish the person would pay more time and affection to you and less to family. If you were attracted to the person's reliable work ethic, now you may wish he or she would not work so hard or so much.

Usually there's enough goodwill and sufficient endorphins left over from the Honeymoon stage that the other person's flaws and idiosyncrasies are brushed over or put to the side. Differences about putting down the toilet seat, keeping makeup off the counter, and making the beds are forgotten in times of connectedness. This connectedness is what we're after—to be felt by another, to be "known" and accepted for who we are and how we are. It's a basic human need we all share and a void we seek to fill. When that need is extreme, we will remain in a deceitful or dishonest relationship in order to keep what we had hoped or thought was a "good" relationship.

Relationships that turn to Disillusionment because of deceitfulness or dishonesty often become discouraging and confusing. Disappointed persons may wonder about their own sanity or ability to make good decisions and about "people picking." Some of us actually have trouble evaluating people because of our family-of-origin issues. Going back to your path of trauma, whether through one-on-one counseling, journaling, or a peer-based support group, is helpful in exploring how those old wounds affect our ability to see and choose people and determine whether an attraction is safe and sane. You may decide to remain free from a romantic relationship until you have worked on those inner issues that keep repeating themselves with new faces.

Communication is also less intense in this second phase of relationship. There may be less frequent and briefer sharing of your thoughts, dreams, and hopes. More negative thoughts and feelings are shared, including more *you shoulds, you coulds,* and *you oughts.* The partners intentionally spend less time together and find other persons to be with who will stroke their limbic and cause them to feel better. In the Disillusionment stage, sex becomes more familiar and less frequent. Over time, such distancing can create a "danger zone," resulting in new emotional connections to others that cause one person to leave the primary relationship behind—emotionally and/or physically. If this becomes a pattern for the one doing the leaving, it can cause a vicious cycle of not feeling good in the primary relationship, looking to others in order to feel good again, and moving further away from the connection once felt in the primary relationship. Trust in the relationship can be permanently damaged.

Adding to these rocky waters are arguments over friends, family, money, priorities, and sex. Often the distancing of the relationship is reflected in the clothing worn to bed, now being sweats, flannels, or other nonexciting bedclothes. During Disillusionment, these differences emerge more often with less agreement on how to solve them. If you want the relationship to evolve, effective communication and solution-focused communication are now essential. However, what tends to happen instead is a movement into the third stage.

Stage 3: Misery
The third stage of relationship is appropriately named "Misery." This is also known as the power struggle, disappointment, or distress stage. You become more aware of the differences between you and your partner and, depending on your style of conflict communication, you find yourself avoiding, accommodating, judging, competing, and fighting in more frequent moments of conflict.

Deep resentments develop at this stage. Issues that may have been annoyances in the Disillusionment stage now become major. Whereas you once saw your partner as absentminded, you now see him or her as uncaring, self-centered, or untrustworthy. Certainly, you conclude, your partner is unable to understand your feelings, or needs.

People know they are in the Misery stage when they begin to ask themselves:

- "Why did I ever get involved with this person in the first place?"
- "What was I thinking?" Or "What was I thinking *with?*"
- "If only I never got involved in the first place."
- "Will this *ever* change?"
- "Is there no way out?"

Couples remain in this stage, building resentments and frustrations, until they decide to do one of the following:

1. End the relationship in some manner.
2. Stay together and continue to avoid the issues (and the person) in the relationship (sometimes for decades).
3. Seek some means to resolve conflicts and pain in the relationship.

Many couples have traveled this same road, from Honeymoon to Disillusionment to Misery, ending their relationships in the Misery stage again and again, and never discovering the possibility of growing the relationship into a fourth stage. This is not because we do not want to grow; it is because we are not taught "how" to take this next step. Without role models of healthy, less conflicting, and more loving relationships, the possibility to do so is limited for many people. So, let's go there now . . . onward to the fourth stage!

My Story of Romantic Relationships

This five-stage model of relationships grew, in part, from watching my mother's behavior with her various boyfriends while I grew up. My mother went through many men after she left my father. Her Honeymoon stage would last until the relationship cooled, and then she'd jump into another Honeymoon with a new man.

From my perspective, my mother's romantic relationships were driven by fear, especially her fear that she could not keep romantic relationships fun and exciting. This made her look for ways to be fun and exciting, fresh and attractive. She did not realize that by doing these "wild things" (drinking, drugging, disappearing) she was sending the message to her partner that she wasn't committed or faithful to the relationship, thereby causing a "self-fulfilling prophecy" and eventually breaking up the relationship.

Later in life, after many relationship trials and errors of my own, including two difficult marriages, I learned that relationships have natural predictable stages. My job is to learn the skills to navigate these stages, not from a place of fear, but using my thinking brain to act deliberately.

Stage 4: Awakening

The Awakening stage in relationship means we wake to the truth in the other person and to our own truth. This is a stage of understanding the emotional fabric of the other, and how it blends and relates to our own fabric. This is also called the stage of stability, friendship, or reconciliation. Couples who make it this far in relationship express feelings of stronger connection, commitment, trust, and love. This is a stage where one learns and accepts that neither of you are perfect creatures, and the truth of this concept is no longer threatening to your self-image.

You both become more confident in your ability to resolve issues, and the two of you develop a process to do so. Unlike the Honeymoon stage, where you only had eyes for each other, or the Disillusionment and Misery stages, where you feared your partner's outside interests, in Awakening, you re-establish your outside interests with the support of your partner.

In this fourth stage of relationship, there is a danger of boredom with your partner, so you need to work harder to maintain the connection. One way is by taking "get-aways." On these occasions, you bring back the intimacy, and perhaps return to places you visited together in your initial Honeymoon stage, reliving some of those same experiences and feelings. The stage of Awakening is evolutionary in that, in order to raise a family and grow old together, at least in a healthy manner, we must learn how to work through the stage of Awakening. It is truly in this stage when we are able to be real, to see the other person as real and intimate to us, and to appreciate, with all the flaws and differences, that this is the person I want to be with . . . no matter what.

Stage 5: Peace and Calm

When a couple does the necessary work (especially if the partners together process the Four Fabulous Agreements exercises coming up next in this chapter), there is a sense of peace that comes with truly knowing each other better, and having accepted certain agreements in order to live and grow together. This fifth stage is also referred to as the stage of commitment, acceptance, transformation, or true love. The essence of this stage is that you are with each other because you have *chosen* each other, faults and all! Your view is that of a partner and a team, an understanding that you will look out for each other's best interests. At this stage, your relationship becomes a true partnership.

The result and reward for the partners is a sense of calmness, the knowledge that they do not have to compete against each other, or the world. They are "there" for each other. Questions they may have once had (*What does he/she want?* or *Where is this relationship going?*) are no longer concerns. In many respects, the Honeymoon has returned to this relationship!

Planning times away together, displaying behaviors of that earlier Honeymoon time (special cards, songs, dinners), wearing fun bed wear (or none at all), and seeking new ways to express your love and adoration for each other—all of this creates a bond that is beyond the usual. You romance each other again! You play and have fun again, laughing and giggling at each other and seeing the humor in the behaviors that once irritated you. The excitement of being with each other is back in the relationship. You text love messages, write on sticky notes and place them around the house or car, and do the things that you know will bring joy and delight. You may even find yourself in the lingerie department of your favorite store looking for that special bedroom clothing meant to excite!

Being in relationship stage 5, Peace and Calm, does not mean there won't be conflict or hurt feelings in the future—it does mean there is a road map to get back on track in your relationship in order to live in love and peace with mutual understanding, respect, and support for one another.

Some Pointers to Remember

Take the following concepts and work on them with your partner. As you work together, "listen with your heart," which means being "present" with the person and hearing what he or she is expressing, without judgment or forming your own response. In this practice of "listening with the heart," it is also vital to learn from each other what each one needs—not wants, but *really needs*—to be in relationship with the other. In other words, what are the "basic needs" for the other person to feel loved, safe, secure, and ready to fully participate in the relationship? This also supports Big Idea 2, not assuming the intent of the other, as agreements have been made that include checking in with the other person when there is misunderstanding.

It takes time and practice to not assume intent, and it takes time to peel away the layers of negative behaviors and trauma and enter into recovery from our past. Like working the Twelve Steps in recovery, we do not go through this process just one time with another person, or even by ourselves. This is an ongoing process as we learn more about our partners, understand more, and stop assuming we know everything about them or their intentions.

As we grow and develop, maturing in our process of recovery, we will cycle through these stages with the significant persons in our lives. The cycles are necessary as we learn more about ourselves and others. We then are willing to remove more layers of beliefs, past behaviors and ideas, and hurts and dig deeper into that core of who we are and what we believe. We will cycle through these stages each time we take a new leap of personal growth. Each time we peel a layer off, there are new insights to be gained and applied. Integration of what we learn along the way is essential to personal change.

Another concept to remember is that one partner can be in the Honeymoon stage while the other partner is in another stage. For example, one person might be in Honeymoon and still feeling magical while the other person is in Disillusionment, wondering what happened to the magic! We will not be at the same stage at the same time until we learn not to assume intentions.

You may have experienced the loss of a relationship because of poor choices, including making assumptions of your partner, assumptions that led to your partner's leaving you because he or she felt the relationship was going nowhere and did not see hope for change. Without hope, there is often no reason to remain in a relationship. Assuming another person's intent decreases the value of the relationship and the other person, often causing him or her to feel that nothing will change for the better, so it's better to get out before wasting time on something that isn't going to work anyway! Carefully consider how long you should stand still in the moment to sort your feelings, and then check them out with your partner (not assuming intent). This is the track to understanding!

Commitment has a hard time growing and deepening without understanding.

Assuming Intent in the Honeymoon Stage

My mother's tendency in a new relationship was to dazzle her romantic target with her beauty and sensuality. Her behavior was predictable. She would invite the new man in her life over to visit, and her self-preparation would include bathing, donning a lovely negligé, pulling her hair back with a beautiful tiara, and applying makeup and perfume. She would answer the door with two drinks in her hands, ready to entertain. This was my role model! So, when I invited my first boyfriend to come over, I went into gear before his arrival, putting on clothes from my mother's closet and applying her makeup and perfume; of course, I prepared two drinks for the visit. Needless to say, when the young boy came to the door and I answered, he had no idea of my intent, nor did I . . . I was just ten years old and following a behavior I'd learned.

There's a lesson here about making assumptions. Other people in our lives may make assumptions about what we mean or who we are based on what they see on the surface. They don't understand or know the context of our behavior. I make assumptions and so does the other party. And, oh, what a party we have sorting through the real intentions from the behavior patterns that we have learned.

As I got older in life, and more mature, I began to ask, specifically, about the context of behaviors and their intent. Finding this out before applying judgment is essential.

An Essential Tool for Big Idea 2: Four Fabulous Agreements

Not assuming intent means that you really don't know what's behind the other person's words or behavior. You have to ask. When you do, an important conversation begins about what you and the other person truly want and need from each other. "Four Fabulous Agreements" is a tool to guide you through this conversation. These are four specific areas to consider when discovering what you and another person need in order to be in relationship with each other. The process of asking questions in these four areas must be entered into without judgment, and with objectivity and openness.

It is helpful to write down your partner's answers, and then switch places and have your partner listen and write. Be open to discovery regarding your responses to the same questions. It is also helpful for the other party not to have to explain his or her answers; simply allow the other person's needs to exist without judgment or criticism.

However, you and your partner should ask follow-up questions when you need clarification, again in a nonjudgmental or leading manner. Decide who will be the listener/recorder first. Prepare for your session by setting the date and time, creating a peaceful environment, and giving yourself plenty of time. This process will help you reach an agreed-upon set of expectations (Four Fabulous Agreements) that will help the two of you develop trust and understanding for each other.

Four Fabulous Agreements

- financial
- physical
- emotional/psychological/social
- spiritual

What If I'm Not Part of a Couple?

If you are not in a romantic relationship, this is still an important exercise to do with yourself in order to know, without influence of endorphins, the issues that really matter to you in each of

these areas. Record your thoughts, knowing that these will be helpful when you approach a new relationship. Keeping on track with
your needs will allow you to be true to yourself and also to clearly
explain them to another person, potentially your future partner.

Financial Agreements

Financial agreements can be tough, as we each grow up with our
own financial philosophy, usually influenced by our family of origin. Some families pass down generational myths and beliefs about
money: how to earn it, how to keep it or use it, who gets to spend
the money, who handles the money, how much money is needed,
and who controls the money.

What is your financial philosophy? Ask these questions of each
other:

- Who works? You, me, or both of us? How many hours of
  each day or each week should be spent working?

- How much money do we each need to make? Are there any
  expectations regarding the amount of income each will earn
  and share?

- How is the money accounted for? In a checkbook? Do we
  each have our own checkbook? Do we have a joint account,
  or do we have a hybrid system (you have your money, I have
  mine, and we have an account for mutual bills)?

- How about savings? What is your financial philosophy about
  saving for something (a vacation, a potentially tough eco-
  nomic period, retirement, children's college tuitions)?

- What are your thoughts about giving to others (charitable
  donations, religious groups, causes you believe in)? Which
  organizations do you prefer to give in-kind donations (tangible goods or service), and which do you prefer to give cash?

- What about credit cards? How do you use them? Do you
  have agreed-upon limits? Do you have a spending limit that

requires agreement from both of you before spending or charging?

By developing a budget for yourself and for the two of you as a couple, you can help keep the arguments (internal or otherwise) to a minimum. Having a budget and sticking to it helps stave off possible character assassinations ("You always spend more than I do!" or "You are so selfish!").

Consider where and how these financial philosophies developed for each of you in your family of origin.

- Was there an attitude that there's "never enough so we better save it all"? Was there no money for fun, extras, or frivolous items? Who decided what was frivolous?

- Was there a belief that no one is to be trusted with money, so everyone must control his or her own money?

- Who taught you what you believe about money and the use of money?

- What rules about money did you grow up with, and how do they play out in your present-day relationships? What were the rules about saving/spending money: how much to save, what's okay to spend money on, and whether it is okay to give money to family members?

- Is it okay to make loans to family members or friends? How much is too much? Do you prefer a written or verbal agreement? What do you do when the person does not pay the loan back?

Much conflict and hurt can be avoided when these issues are discussed and agreed upon. A clear set of expectations for oneself and others can be established with non-blame and non-shame standards and principles. Finance is a heavy issue that takes a lot of discussion when money is short or new expenses come into the picture, or even when new desires arise for items that are beyond the current budget. Keeping a budget and tracking your income and expenses gives both partners a sense of where they are with money and where they are going. Budgets also enable you to plan for future needs or desires. There's less to argue about with an agreed-upon budget.

Physical Agreements

Life gives us many choices regarding our physical needs and agreements when two people are in relationship. At certain points in our lives, it's hard to believe there are other considerations besides the sexual side of physical. But let's start there:

- What are your expectations for the frequency of physical sexual expression?
- What are your expectations and needs for the physical expression of cuddling?
- What types of physical sexual expressions are acceptable to you, including sexual positions and use of "toys"?
- Is sexual activity strictly between the two of you, or is the addition of others acceptable to you?
- Do you have certain things that are important or helpful in preparing ahead of time, like bathing, general grooming, birth control, room temperature, and any other environmental factors?
- Are there certain things that assist you in "getting in the mood"?

What is your philosophy about the purpose of sexual activity?
- It is tied to having children only.
- It is to be done only with certain conditions met.
- It should not be too much fun, too strict, too sensual, too reserved . . . any of the "toos."

- Sex is reserved for marriage, committed relationships, or other beliefs.
- Sex for sex alone is okay, not okay, or it depends.

Other areas to consider in the physical realm:

- What creates physical safety for you?
- What are appropriate body boundaries in your intimate relationships?
- A "body bubble" is the space around us that we either allow others to enter or not. Are there times when you feel more accepting of physical activity within your body bubble and other times not?

There are also expectations about how we care for ourselves, including grooming, exercise, and nutrition.

- What are your expectations for your own and your partner's hygiene, grooming, and general self-care? Do you have a philosophy about seeing dentists and doctors for regular checkups?
- What is your personal philosophy regarding exercise and general health?
- What level and amount of time spent exercising do you consider acceptable?
- How does nutrition play into your eating habits? What about alcohol and other drugs, sweets, and fatty foods?
- How does smoking fit into your physical expectations?

Space is another area that's important to the physical expectations of relationships. Consider the following:

- What type and amount of physical space do you need to live in comfort?

- Do you prefer a home with lots of furnishings or do you prefer a home with fewer furnishings?
- Do you prefer city life or country life?
- Do you prefer a hot or cold climate?
- What style of furniture do you like—contemporary, antique, country, a mix?
- What type of bed do you like to sleep in? Double, queen, or king size? Hard, soft, waterbed?

Each of these areas presents a potential conflict and grounds for arguments that can affect the relationship. Being clear and reaching agreements on these areas can lead a relationship back from discord to mutual benefit and enjoyment.

Body Bubbles Rise on Different Occasions

Because of the sexual abuse I experienced, there are times that my body has an "untimely" response to a sexual situation. For no apparent reason, my body feels overwhelmed by the intimacy, I begin to feel smothered, and the weight of my spouse feels confining. It is a body memory reaction that rises from within. At those times, I have learned to talk to my limbic and remind myself that I am in a different situation with a person I love and have agreed to be sexual with, and that no harm is coming to me. However, if the feeling is too great, I have made an agreement with my husband that he will move away from me when I ask him to, without a question and without feeling that I am being unkind to him. We are aware that this body bubble issue can arise, and we know how to deal with it without blame or shame to each other.

Emotional/Psychological/Social Agreements

Emotional, psychological, and social considerations are part of how we relate intimately with each other. When we feel emotionally cared for, psychologically boosted, and socially involved with our partner, we have more mutual trust and support for each other. Emotional and psychological support may mean different things to each person. Social support depends on the partners' needs, as well as the history they bring from their family of origin and the relationships they have experienced to date. The "wellness" of these past relationships and family supports may determine the level of support the person currently needs. Developing a reciprocal set of agreements in these areas will lead to an understanding of each person's emotional strengths and challenges.

Consider the following in determining your needs and agreements in this area:

- Are certain situations (times of the year, seasons) more difficult emotionally or psychologically? This could be related to a loss (death, divorce, accident, or change in life).

- When does your partner feel he or she needs more support from you? In what type of situations? Are there different circumstances that require specific types of support? Answer these questions for yourself as well.

- When does your partner just want you to listen and (possibly) hold them, rub their back, or just be "present" with them? When do you do this?

- What do you need for positive emotional and psychological support? What does your partner need?

- Do you expect unconditional love and support? Do you know how to give that to others? If not, are you willing to learn?

- Do you expect to be listened to—to have your pain and hurts taken seriously? Do you do that for others?

- How does that play out at the end of a long day, a tough weekend, or after an argument? Do you hold that agitated feeling (e.g., anger toward the boss, coworkers, or family members) close, or do you work to release it? Do you pull it back to use at another time, like a defensive weapon?

- Do you allow yourself or others to walk away during an argument? How do you agree to close the argument down in order to find solutions later? What needs do you have for finding resolution?

Social needs are also important—how we relate socially in our own separate worlds, and in the world we create with our partner. This is also relevant to how we find mutual enjoyment outside of each other's company.

- What are your social expectations, and how do you see your partner relating to those in a reciprocal manner? This includes going out together or separately, the frequency of social occasions, the gender of friends, or the degree of intimacy acceptable in social relationships. Do you always need to be together when going to a social event? What boundaries do you find acceptable?

- Do you have a desire for social involvement often? Does your partner? What happens when your views do not match?

- Is your partner secure in a social situation? Are you? How do you support each other when one or the other does not feel secure?

- Where do previous relationships fall into your social, emotional, and psychological needs and agreements? Do you have an agreement about socializing with exes?

Spiritual Agreements

Spirituality means different things to different people. Some people feel they do not have a "spiritual" side to themselves. In this area, we are not necessarily discussing religion. The spiritual area we are concerned with is the sense of self that goes beyond our own intellectual self, that sense that there is a power greater than ourselves. In recovery, we call this our Higher Power. It is expressed in different ways, and the key to this agreement is to learn how you and your partner express a sense of the spiritual.

Other considerations to understand for self or partner in the spiritual area are as follows:

- What does spirituality mean to you? How do you currently, or in the future, want to express it?
- In what ways do you desire for your partner to be involved?
- Where do you receive your source of external strength? How do you prefer to express it?
- Are reading, praying, worship, music, dance, or other activities involved in this expression?
- Do you want to express your spirituality with another? To what degree?
- If you have children, do you want spirituality to be part of their lives? What agreements are important to you in the context of children?
- What are your other spiritual expectations?
- What occasions are spiritually special? Do you want to recognize these occasions in a specific manner?

As individuals understand this area for themselves and their partners, they can decide if they can and want to meet a partner's spiritual needs. There might be other items that one or the other partner "wants." These can be negotiated as well.

"I'm Not a Spiritual Person"

I have clients who tell me they have no sense of a spiritual self. I ask them, "Have you ever had a desperate moment or time in your life?" Everyone has had that moment. I then ask, "What changed that feeling for you? Was it something you read, someone you talked to or prayed to, or a certain place you went to, like the ocean, the mountains, or a desert, that brought you to a better place? What would you say caused you to change to a more hopeful feeing?" Once they tell this story to me, or to themselves, I find that they can gauge whether this was a place or situation where they discovered a sense of spirituality.

After You've Completed the Four Areas of Agreement

Once these four areas have been discussed, you and your partner can negotiate an agreement for each area and then write it down. (See the Four Fabulous Agreements exercise.) Considering the difference between "needs" and "wants" in a relationship will help you to determine priorities in setting the agreements. These agreements might also be written down in the form of a contract and signed by both parties. Putting an agreement in a picture frame and placing it on a dresser may be a reminder for each of you. Having it close by is helpful when a dispute begins to arise— a quick "let's-take-a-minute-to-consider-our-agreement" moment may divert a full-blown argument.

Four Fabulous Agreements Example

Financial

- Agree to not spend more than $50 in cash, credit, or debit without the agreement of the other person on the item.
- Agree to keep a budget and review it monthly with each other, planning for our vacation by setting aside $150 per month.
- Agree to pay all of our bills on time, with bills as the priority before any extras.

Physical

- Agree to play in a sexual manner with each other weekly, or several times per week.
- Agree to work out, together or separately, an average of three times per week.
- Agree to be mindful of our food intake, eating more fresh fish, fruit, and veggies.
- Agree to save money to buy a bed that we both like.

Social/Psychological/Emotional

- Agree to spend time at a party together and introduce each other to our friends.
- Agree to not go out with the guys or girls more than twice a week.
- Agree to have our own "date night" every week.
- Agree to be thoughtful of the rough times in each of our days by listening to each other when we both get home.

Spiritual

- Agree to read a couples devotional nightly.
- Agree to pray a prayer together daily.
- Agree to meditate at a peaceful place weekly.
- Agree to give to others through donations of cash, food, clothing, and time.

Review the four agreements on a regular basis. People change, and understanding that agreements can change is a healthy way to grow in your relationship.

If we apply our understanding of conflict communication styles to be more supportive of the relationship, if we use the stages of relationships model to gain insights into where our relationship is at, and if we work through our differences with a partner using the Four Fabulous Agreements, then we will find little left to assume.

Four Fabulous Agreements Exercise

In your own words, describe the agreements you've made in each of the four areas with yourself and, if in a relationship, with the other person.

Financial

_____

_____

_____

_____

Physical

_____

_____

_____

_____

Emotional/Psychological/Social

_____

_____

_____

_____

Spiritual

_____

_____

_____

_____

BIG IDEA 3

Dig Deeper into the Conflict

Each new Big Idea for reining in your brain builds on the one before it, so let's take a moment to review Big Ideas 1 and 2.

Big Idea 1 advises us to *stand still in the moment*. We invoke this concept when we are about to make a fight-or-flight decision driven by fear or anger. It reminds us to be deliberate in our decisions, to move our thought process to the frontal cortex, and to consider our style of conflict—whether we're about to use a reactionary style (compete, accommodate, or avoid) or a more functional style (compromise or collaborate).

Big Idea 2 cautions us to *not assume intent* and to avoid jumping to conclusions. It encourages us to understand the stages of relationships in order to be more thoughtful. It reminds us to ask our partners (and others) to explain their intent rather than to project our own view onto their motives. It encourages us to learn more about others and build a positive relationship through understanding the four areas of agreement that govern relationships, particularly a romantic bond.

In this chapter, Big Idea 3 tells us to *dig deeper into the conflict*. The concept of digging deeper stems from the belief that when another person's behavior is defensive or offensive, the issue is often more complex than what appears on the surface. Quite often this deeper issue involves the other person's family of origin, or it connects to baggage carried forward from an earlier relationship.

This skill of digging beyond the obvious to discover a deeper issue encourages us to keep in mind the best interest of the other person rather than focusing only on our own feelings. By considering the other person's needs, you are willing to build the other person's "emotional bank account." You are supporting the relationship by requesting more information, listening with your heart, and suspending your responses while you gather your thoughts and deliberate on your response. "What does it take to do this?" you may ask. Your best response to relationship conflict will draw from a combination of concepts. Let's begin with the process of identifying feelings—your own and those of the other person.

How Do I Know How I'm Really Feeling?

The identification of feelings is sometimes difficult. Some people's feelings are "frozen" because of trauma or addiction, or because when they were growing up they never learned how to connect with their emotions. In some families, being male means never showing your feelings, and being female means showing them with little restraint. Often, we respond to a distressing situation by saying "I'm so angry!" or "I'm so mad!" when what we are really feeling is hurt, confusion, or something else.

Accurately identifying feelings in a situation will help you and others dig deeper to discover the actual feeling at hand. Doing so will train your thinking brain to use deliberate words and actions. Only then will you be able to speak to and resolve the real issue driving the conflict you are experiencing.

Faces and Feelings

Years ago, therapists and counselors used images of faces exhibiting different expressions to help clients see and identify deeper feelings. Below is an inventory of many of those feelings. Please take a minute to visualize the face you see yourself or others making when you read the corresponding word. Place these words in your thinking brain to draw from in the future.

Confused	Exhausted	Ecstatic	Guilty
Sad	Frustrated	Hysterical	Hostile
Happy	Confident	Embarrassed	Mischievous
Ashamed	Enraged	Frightened	Disgusted
Cautious	Smug	Depressed	Overwhelmed
Hateful	Love struck	Lonely	Hopeful
Jealous	Bored	Anxious	Surprised
Irritated	Shy	Zealous	Shocked
Agitated	Caring	Empathic	Loving

We each have different amounts of "emotional energy" we are willing and able to extend to others. This is determined by our own emotional ability and what we believe the other person is "due."

Some people learned in their family of origin to withhold emotion (Avoider). If we remain unaware of the conflict communication style we adopted earlier in life, we may wonder why we now have trouble connecting with another person or remaining in a relationship for the long term. Others have learned to adjust to someone else's needs to the point of giving up their own identity (Accommodator). Some people have learned to emotionally push their way in and around the relationship (Competer), even if it means "beating the other person up" verbally.

Why Did I Choose My Partner?

There are positive and healthy reasons to be attracted to and develop a relationship with someone, and there are less healthy reasons for doing so.

Some people bond over a cause they're both fighting *against,* like war or poverty. Other people fight *for* something, such as clean air or water, or a particular political candidate. Issues such as these can unite two people to such a degree that personal differences can be glossed over. However, when the cause ends for one or both, so do many relationships founded on that cause. This is also seen in relationships that spring out of Twelve Step groups, when people get together out of their shared cause of staying sober. Often if one person relapses, the other is influenced to do the same. This does not mean you shouldn't be with a person if you both believe in the same things. The challenge is reframing the relationship beyond your shared cause.

Some people bond over a shared personal goal. This could be an educational goal, like graduating from college together. Or it could be an athletic goal. When a relationship is based solely on something you are doing together, there is no foundation on which to continue the relationship once the goal is accomplished. This could also be said about relationships based on crisis, or financial gain, or a shared workplace. The question of durability comes up once any of those circumstances changes. Then what happens to the relationship? A relationship is better when it is based on a combination of attractions, such as common values, beliefs, goals, worldviews, and life direction. The foundation of any healthy romantic relationship is a good friendship. This involves working past the Honeymoon stage until you are in the Awakening stage and begin to see the person in his or her entirety. Then, a mindful decision can be made about whether the two of you are a "good fit." When your endorphins are raging, there is little mindfulness or clear determination about shared values. When approaching the decision of whether this person may become more than a Honeymoon attraction, the Four Fabulous Agreements presented previously can be discussed to learn more about each other and discover where you match and where you do not.

What Does an Unhealthy Relationship Look Like?

Frequently, the dynamics from our family of origin prevent us from knowing the difference between healthy and unhealthy relationships in adulthood. Most people strive for healthy relationships but grow up without a gauge with which to recognize one when they see it—or are already in it. Often, overarching unhealthy behaviors learned in families are passed down from one generation to another. Here are some examples of unhealthy behaviors:

- The **attempt to control** what the other person does, who she sees, how he dresses, what she believes. Controlling another person is not necessary when and if you have common values and beliefs and you have made agreements regarding basic behaviors and boundaries. Controlling becomes a wedge in the relationship that eventually pushes the couple apart.

- **Negative manipulation** is another unhealthy behavior. "Positive manipulation" happens when you keep the best interests of another in mind. The problem occurs when manipulative behavior is not done for the highest good of the other person—when it meets the need of the manipulator instead. The other difference between the two is that positive manipulation is not pushed upon the other person; it is offered as an alternative or reasonable choice—*choice* being the operative word.

- A **"you-owe-me" attitude** also tears down a relationship. People develop this attitude based on what they have learned from family or society. It is a belief that one does something for someone else based solely on getting something from that person in return. This behavior does not take into consideration that a person may do something for another with no expectation of getting something in return. The difficulty with a you-owe-me attitude is that it is not always clear when someone has this expectation, nor when the person will require payment. It makes it hard to give or receive tokens of gratitude or affection without feeling like there are obligations involved. It is healthier to have such an agreement up front and out in the open.

What Does a Healthy Relationship Look Like?

Regardless of what role you may have adopted previously in relationship conflicts, at this point, I ask you to consider holding a new, healthy worldview. What would that be like? It would mean having a view of relationships that looks something like this:

- **Being with someone—*no matter what.*** This does not mean you agree to stay with a person who is mean, hateful, or hurtful. It does mean being in a relationship with the knowledge that there are going to be tough times, times when you will want to run, or times when your attention (or desire) wants to take you in other directions. You agree (within yourself and with your partner) that this is a person you are going to stick with, and find new ways to communicate and live with. You agree to dig deeper into the issues that build a wall between the two of you. Again, while a love relationship often provides the most vivid picture of these issues, this could also relate to a parent relationship, a friendship, or an employer/employee relationship. It is a way of thinking that honors the relationship and puts each of you in a stance where you do not run at the first (or tenth) hint of hurt.

- **We are *interdependent* on each other—interconnected.** We need each other. This view recognizes that there are different ways to connect with others. We can be dependent on someone, we can be independent, or we can be interdependent, where we allow the influence of others as well as our own worldview to shape our lives. When we take an interdependent stance in relationship, we recognize that, as human beings, we need each other. This does not mean we are weak or selfless. In healthy relationships, we change our focus from *me* to *we* and express this interrelatedness in thoughts, words, and behaviors.

- **Relationships are entered into with heart and soul, without worrying about the *outcome*.** You may have grown up learning that you must always have a "backup plan" in case the relationship does not work out. The difficulty with this way of thinking is that when we have a backup plan, we do not truly invest our all in the relationship. There are pieces held back or given in another direction, maybe to another person, and the primary relationship cannot be entered into with heart and soul. Many of us learned in our families of origin not to trust in a relationship because it will eventually fail, so we automatically put less energy into the relationship, thereby causing the relationship to fail due to lack of investment. Instead, in a healthy relationship, our thoughts move to thinking (and eventually believing) that this relationship will have a positive outcome! We visualize that the outcome will be positive because the actions and thought processes are from our frontal cortex; thus, we are deliberate in our intention to be considerate and proactive in the relationship, and not just waiting to "see where it goes." We're actually directing the course of the relationship using the Big Ideas we're learning here.

- **All you want is *the other person's* highest good.** This concept may sound counterintuitive. Your limbic may be screaming out "What about me? My highest good!" Not to worry, your limbic will be soothed by the positive results of thinking about another person's needs, because the reality is that your limbic will be on watch for you—even while your cortex is directing the action. We all tend to be *me* centered; now, we think in the direction of the other person and whether his or her highest good is being considered or factored into the relationship. This is especially helpful for the Avoider and Competer types among us, in that we have a tendency not to look toward the needs of others. (The Avoider tends not to look at his own needs, either.)

- **You are willing to do what is right to *rescue* the relationship.** To rescue is to throw out a lifeline when someone is drowning or to help a person who has no means to get out of a difficult situation. Of course, we like to think we would rescue someone in a life-threatening situation. But what about people in an emotionally or psychologically threatening situation? Are we as apt to assist them? Or do we stand to the side to measure what it means for us before we assist? In this alternative, healthier view of relationships, we operate on the premise that the relationship has value and so does the other person. We believe the person deserves our support and assistance in moving through a difficult emotional/psychological situation. This does not mean we allow ourselves to be forever rescuing that person or giving of ourselves in a sacrificial manner. Balance is the key to this view, especially for the Accommodator, who tends to help others at the expense of his or her own needs.

- **It is not what happened, but *what you do with what happened.*** So often our limbic is stuck on what happened in a given situation, especially if it had a negative effect on us. Sometimes our reactions (avoid, accommodate, and compete) actually contribute to the negative effects of what happened. Nothing is really solved, blame and shame run high, and we all walk away from the situation feeling helpless and unable to solve the problem. In a healthier relationship stance, we take the view that negative things happen in life, even when we plan to make things positive. We believe that, together, we are going to find a way to move this negative situation to a more hopeful place. Approaching life and relationships with this view gives both people more power. When we approach negative life situations as a Collaborator, we look for mutual needs, mutual understanding, and the mutual win. It is not a black-and-white approach that says, "Either you are going to win, or I am going to win." Together, using two minds working from the cortex, the two of you will more likely find a solution that feels like a win for both of you.

- **Doing all this means *taking risks.*** Yes, relationships are risky. You can get hurt. Yet the biggest danger you face is if you base the relationship on *me.* Throughout this book, we examine how easy it is to be *me* centered. Moving to *we* is a risk. It may also be new for us, making it unfamiliar and sometimes awkward. It takes time to train the brain to think and live in this way. Our task is to build a third reaction—beyond fight or flight. This third reaction requires that we stop in the moment of conflict and consider the *we* as a "center of gravity" from which all paths lead.

- **It requires the ability to *forgive.*** Being able to forgive is key to being happy with others and ourselves. Are there things in life that are hard to forgive and justify? Yes. There are things that seem larger than life or, in a word, unforgivable. It is our choice what we hold on to. We must decide what we wish to hold on to and what we will try to forgive. The more we can let go, the lighter our emotional/psychological load. We could spend the whole book on this issue alone; suffice it to say, forgiving is hard, but not letting go of hurt is harder still.

Using Big Idea 3 to Achieve a Healthier Relationship

Have you ever incurred the wrath of an angry person and thought, "Wow! That's clearly an overreaction! I wonder what is causing so much anger." Or, conversely, have you ever had an intense and powerful reaction to what someone did or said and thought, "Wow! That was an intense feeling I just had. Where did that come from?" When we've been in a conflict and a memory is evoked (either through words, behaviors, or feelings), we may think, "I thought I was done with those feelings! I wonder why my emotions are flooding with this old stuff now."

These circumstances happen to us every day. Sometimes anger and conflict are fueled by past psychological, emotional, or physical abuse. Added to that are the layers of unresolved emotions from past relationships: hurt, pain, feeling devalued or embarrassed, and many others. We become skilled at hiding our vulnerability—even from ourselves! Denial is common, while being in touch with feelings is less familiar to many of us. We use our limbic system to keep vulnerable feelings well hidden from others as *protection,* or so we believe. However, without an ability to access our emotions, we put ourselves in greater danger, since layers of denial deaden our emotional capacity *and* our ability to control our impulses.

Next, we will identify methods to dig deeper into a conflict in order to learn what may be hiding behind anger or emotionally overloaded expressions. Digging deeper into conflict and anger is like being an archaeologist in three important ways: It requires hard work, it takes time and care, and it raises expectations of finding some type of treasure if we keep digging. Treasure, in the case of relationships, is something that enriches the "fabric" of our lives. It reaches into past individual or family experiences, and any unresolved grief we're carrying for ourselves or for past generations, as well as the happiness and love we feel within ourselves and for generations past.

Becoming an archaeologist in this context requires an understanding that each person can feel and behave both wonderfully and desperately. This is not a "judgment dig" or a comparison game to determine whose pain is worse, or whose life is better. It is more like a "reality show" starring the persons we are attempting to know better. It is their reality. The more we put our own assumptions aside and simply watch their "show," the faster we can determine the real issues underlying a heated exchange.

Being an archaeologist in a disagreement or conflict is a process of digging until we learn what caused a heated response in the other person, when the situation seemed to call for something more reasonable. After all, you were only discussing where to go for dinner, weren't you? Or were you? Digging deeper goes beyond a surface discussion about dinner. It moves the two of you into the layers of disappointment or hurt that may be lurking underneath a seemingly neutral topic. This pain may not even be caused by the current relationship, but is left over from a past relationship. In this case, you may be a stand-in for a former partner. You may have used certain words, behaviors, or mannerisms that brought this unresolved issue to the surface, not meaning to do so. This is the time to "back up the train" and dig deeper, while not bringing any assumptions, shame, or blame into the discussion.

What follows is a method that may help make digging deeper more fruitful. Give yourselves time for a discussion without interruptions, and choose a relaxing environment. Bring paper and pen. Changing the way we do things, indeed changing the brain, is a thoughtful process. By writing things down and considering them later, we keep breakthroughs and insights in mind for future use.

This raises another important aspect of how people change. We need to "do" the new behavior before we can "believe" the behavior. As discussed previously, we are changing the neuropathways in our brains, and this process takes repetition and thought. Writing things down helps us achieve this goal.

Charting Past and Present "Deeper Issues"

Sit with your partner next to you in a private place. Each of you take a sheet of paper and draw a line down the center to create two columns. At the top of one column, write the heading "Before." Label the other column "After." In the Before column, list any past psychological, emotional, physical, social, and financial abuses you have experienced that still affect this relationship. Examples include a physically abusive father, or an ex-wife who abandoned you and emptied your bank account. You will each have your own past abuses and deeper issues that are carried over.

In the After column, record unresolved issues within your present relationship. Examples might include the tendency of one partner to run up charges on a credit card without consulting the other, or one person's "anger problem," manifested by yelling first and asking questions later. Identify what was said or done, and what each of you would like to take back.

Share your Before and After lists. Discuss how the Before issues come up unexpectedly in the After issues, even when they're not related to the current situation. Decide how to support each other when this occurs; for example, you might use a word or phrase that allows the other person to know that past issues are creeping into current issues. Agree to take the time to discover the past issues your current problems are tied to so that you do not connect them incorrectly to your current partner—unless they belong there too. Work through how the two of you will repair these issues in order to avoid accidental collisions in the future. Again, the goal is not to make these issues disappear. It is to adopt new ways of dealing with them using intention and practice. With time, these issues will become resolved.

Each of us carries feelings of displaced hurt and anger, disappointment, and frustration left over from incidents in the past, whether they happened in our childhood or that very morning! For example, the boss tells us, in so many words, that our idea is not good enough. That criticism brings forth feelings of rejection we experienced in childhood. We carry and hide our pain until we get home or reach a place where we feel safe. Then, if our partner criticizes us for forgetting to take out the garbage, we become huffy or sarcastic. The problem is that we not only exist in this point in time. There are emotional areas where our defensive layers may be thin, where the veneer is worn through. When those areas are triggered by current events, we can easily say and do things that we later regret.

If put into practice, Big Idea 3, Dig Deeper into the Conflict, can prevent us from "going there." For example, people often find themselves arguing about trivial things, like what to watch on TV. Two people might argue about this for some time, until one or the other says, "I just don't care! Do what you want to—you always do!" When an argument arrives at this point, the real issue of contention is not the choice of one program over another. It is a leftover, unresolved argument—perhaps an argument they had the night before over finances. As such, it is displaced anger.

When couples think back to their angriest and most painful fights, they often do not recall what started the argument. There may have been a theme to these arguments—finances, sex, children, work, time together, loss of respect or love. The argument likely started over a trivial issue and then blew up because of a backlog of unresolved feelings and issues. The surface issue becomes the proverbial straw that broke the camel's back or, as I like to say, the "tick, tick, BOOM" reaction.

At the same time, these disputes, such as arguing over who will make dinner or whose turn it is to wash dishes, are not unimportant to the relationship. Surface issues can function as catalysts to vent each person's deeper pain and frustration. We all need to blow off pressure sometimes and somewhere. For most of us, it seems safer to do this at home rather than with others in our work or social environments. So we explode at home because we assume that forgiveness will be there. It is taken for granted! This isn't likely to change, but we can change how we respond to the overreactions of our partners.

For many people, especially Competers, every conflict presents itself as a black-or-white, win-or-lose situation. Either I take control and get what I want, or you do. An outcome where we both get what we want does not seem possible. However, by digging deeper and listening with our hearts to what may be behind the other person's thoughts, feelings, and behaviors might open the door to revelations of a deeper treasure of possibilities and potential.

The more we dig deeper to learn what is underneath the surface, the more likely we are to get to the real issues. Day-to-day sharing of feelings and frustrations helps to keep things in perspective. Dealing with conflict as it appears, and resolving what is real and what is left over from the past, allows us to respect and honor each person. We may fear that it will be too painful to dig deeper and look for our partner's past pain; however, when one of us holds on to that pain, it can produce much deeper hurt—for both of us. Listening with our hearts opens the other person to trust our willingness to solve the conflict together. Once we sort out what is a real issue versus a surface irritation, and after the two of us make an agreement about how we're going to handle the issue differently in the future, we can put the relationship back on course. We may even get to enjoy a romantic dinner together instead of spending the night alone in separate bedrooms.

Healthy and Unhealthy Relationship Exercise

Think back on your significant past relationships. Make a table listing each relationship, its healthy qualities, and its unhealthy qualities. Consider the healthy qualities you want to add from the information you have learned thus far (e.g., resolving conflict by talking it through, listening with your heart, weekly date nights) and add those to your healthy qualities. Consider the unhealthy qualities you want to discard from your behaviors (e.g., jumping to conclusions, shouting your way through an argument, walking out the door in a huff, saying yes when you mean no) and make an agreement with yourself to work on letting those go.

Moving closer and more consistently to the healthy qualities will grow and mature you, causing you to be more content with yourself and others to be more content with you as well. Moving away from unhealthy behaviors will cause the same. Changing those specific behaviors through awareness and deliberate thoughtfulness are positive recovery processes to invest in that pay huge emotional rewards.

>> Table on next page

Healthy and Unhealthy Relationship

Past Relationship	Healthy Qualities	Unhealthy Qualities

BIG IDEA 4
Cultivate Confusion

There are two basic ways of engaging someone in conflict. You can come at your "opponent" by kicking the door down with proverbial guns blazing. Or you can meet the other person calmly, openly, and assertively, leaving your blame at the door. The aggressive approach, the technique used primarily by Competers, is not likely to be successful, at least not in the long run, because it leaves both parties wounded.

Think longer term. Taking a defensive stance in conflict puts others in the position of an enemy who will work against you every chance they get, while a cooperative approach creates an ally who will work with you as a team member. This is the path more often used in mutual problem-solving/solution-focused techniques. Earlier, we named such people Collaborators. That's what we need to be if we wish to live more thoughtfully in recovery—less centered in our limbic, and more in our cortex, in thoughts, words, and deeds.

The other four conflict communication styles—avoiding, competing, compromising, and accommodating—do not help us engage in mutual problem solving. Even the Compromiser fails to fully honor the feelings and needs of the other person in conflict.

One of the most powerful tools for resolving conflicts is to *be in confusion*. Remaining willfully confused about a conflict or a hurtful situation and withholding judgment allows for a situation in which no one is blamed or shamed. It also helps you collect and share information to shed more light on the deeper issues behind heated words or actions. Then, one party does not have to go with first impressions or immediate feelings of hurt or disappointment. Instead, the person keeps emotions in neutral and looks for further explanation. This creates a much more open and productive atmosphere to support the resolution of conflict.

Allowing yourself to remain confused gives you time to develop an understanding of the other person's motives or, as I like to call it, the totality of someone's being—the person's fabric. As discussed around Big Idea 2, Do Not Assume Intent, we often think the worst about a situation, and the person who has hurt us. As an extreme illustration of "worst-case" thinking, picture a weekend where your partner has opted to spend the afternoon without you. In your disappointment, you might imagine his thought process going along these lines:

"I am going to play tennis with my friend on Saturday just because I want to frustrate my wife and cause her to feel lonely and unappreciated."

Is this a rational response? Of course not, but if we're honest with ourselves, it's not too far off from what we often think. More than likely our partner has quite a different motive for leaving us out of his Saturday plans. Perhaps he needs to burn off energy after a frustrating workweek, and he chooses to release that energy in an aggressive tennis match rather than bringing it home to you.

Making assumptions about another person's true intentions is dangerous business. The best way to learn someone's true motives is to ask questions in a neutral, nonthreatening manner that focuses on gathering information.

Often in our family of origin, we did not learn ways to suspend judgment; we did not learn the words or phrases that can change the direction of a conversation from hostile or competitive to neutral. These are learned words and sentences. Once we place these in our frontal cortex, we can retrieve them.

Things to Say to Help *Cultivate Confusion*

- "I am confused. Earlier, did you mean that you wanted to do it this way, and now you are changing your mind and you would like to do it another way instead?"

- "I am confused. Did we not have an agreement to do_____? Please help me understand this change."

- "Help me understand why I am feeling this resistance. Did I say or do something to offend you?"

- "It feels like we have moved from a rational conversation to a hurtful conversation. Do you feel this as well or am I just confused?"

- "Help me understand how we can move away from this impasse to a place of more positive growth."

- "I'm confused. It felt like we were connected and in agreement on this issue before. What happened since we last spoke about it? Did you change your mind?"

- To find out someone's intentions using Big Idea 4, you might say, "I'm confused. Is this what you intended?" or in a conflict, "I'm confused. How did we get to this place of anger? I wonder if we can find another way to solve this?"

It is amazing how two people can perceive the same situation or issue differently, regardless of how long they have been together. Over time, couples may jump to conclusions about each other's behavior almost instantly instead of putting those assumptions on hold until more information is collected. This can lead to the sort of bickering that subverts many long-term relationships and marriages. Although common, this habit—equal parts assuming intent and not cultivating confusion—is both negative and self-indulgent.

In conflict situations, our first thoughts are often totally off the mark because of the strong emotions in play. It is important to stay consistent in reminding ourselves to gather information from its source before our own interpretation becomes totally entrenched. Our personal investment in our own truth about a situation may stand in the way of receiving new information that challenges our conclusions.

The faster we make a judgment—without collecting information or suspending our thoughts and allowing ourselves to be confused—the less likely we will find other possibly truer motives. The more pain and/or hurt you feel, the more distorted your perceptions are likely to be, and the more you'll be tempted to hold on to your defensiveness as you engage in self-pity.

Practicing Confusion as a Couple

The practice of confusion is a great tool for couples working on their relationship because, in general, people have a low tolerance for confusion. Our natural survival instincts push us toward certainty—whether we're right or wrong. The longer we are in relationship with someone, the more certain we feel we know the person, and the less room we give him or her to change. Being confused about another person's behavior seems counterintuitive at this point in the relationship. However, part of respecting our partner is not believing we know him or her so well that we cannot be confused. Giving individuals we are close to the ability to change their behavior before our eyes is a gift to them and to ourselves. Uncertainty is uncomfortable in a culture that prefers and promotes black-and-white answers. We may have spent our lives projecting an image of ourselves as someone who knows exactly what we are thinking and talking about. In a relationship, this can be especially challenging. Our partner may challenge what we know and believe to be true. We may make incorrect assumptions about our partner's beliefs and motives.

Being confused is an honorable and productive way of going public with our vulnerability. Granted, it may feel safer (at first) to lead with our *invulnerability*, holding on to a façade of sureness or cool aloofness. However, our load becomes lighter when we admit that we are imperfect creatures, not flawless superhumans. We are also much more fun to be around once we take off the armor that accompanies the need to be right or perfect. Packing fewer offensive and defensive weapons opens us up to the joys of intimacy and closeness.

Being confused is actually a powerful state to be in, both for ourselves and others. No blame or shame is distributed, as it has not been decided what or who is to blame. For the moment, no one feels like they have to defend themselves. For the moment, everyone involved has an opportunity to move to mutual solutions resulting in mutual benefits.

Help with Cultivating Confusion

We all need some assistance in solving our relationship issues. When we become angry or frustrated and try to force our solution on another, we become more isolated and receive less help. We expend more energy as we try to create a *me* answer, not a *we* answer to the issue. Since the other person was not consulted, he or she automatically resists being controlled. Would you?

There is a more effective step in the process of drawing another person into creating a *we* solution, and that is the practice of collecting information rather than dispensing solutions. An angry person dispenses information about all the things others should/could/would do differently. A proactive person collects information by saying things like "I'm confused." "We have something we need to solve." "What ideas would you suggest to help this situation?" "Is there something that you could commit to doing to help me or that we could do together to resolve this issue?" This openness helps build on the other person's ideas rather than forcing them to accept our own thoughts and solutions.

Solid Decision Making in Relationships

Decision making by two or more people in a relationship (a couple, family members, neighbors, a team of coworkers) is best done when certain steps are taken. Not all decisions require all of these steps, although any critical or complex decision is best decided after some work is done using this approach.

This process can be done solo or with others. Doing these steps with others helps to inform us of other ways of thinking. Consider that the more people you bring into this process (especially when the decision concerns a workplace or neighborhood), the richer the process will be and the greater "buy-in" you will receive from others involved. If the issue is of a personal nature, including those close to you offers them an opportunity to be part of the *we* and builds collaboration in the relationship. Living and thinking outside our own brains does open us to the richness of living and thinking with others.

Effective Decision-Making Steps

- Identify what you and others believe to be the true issue. Sometimes this is the most difficult task. We may focus on one issue, when something else is in fact the primary issue. Asking others what they see as the primary matter at hand is helpful to viewing the problem from all sides. Being open and transparent gives way to more reflection by others in looking at the situation.

- Look at and list all solutions. Our minds can become stuck on doing something one way only. "That is the way we have always done it" is heard just as often in staff meetings as family discussions. Taking the time to think about all possible options, whether seemingly feasible or not, may lead to a better, hybrid option.

- Speak with others about the options listed. Gather more ideas on how to look at the real issue and ideas to resolve it. Use technology to find out if this same issue has been discovered, discussed, and solved by others. There are many forums and online resources for parents, couples, managers, etc. Speak with others who have experienced the same issue. Write down their thoughts and your own opinion about their solution.

- Review all options and check out the potential consequences. Discuss potential consequences with others to see if you are missing anything. Decide which consequences you can live with or which might be less problematic.

- Choose the top decision—not what *you* want to do, but what makes the most sense to both of you or the team. It should be the most collaborative (*we*) if it is going to be the best solution for the long term.

- Execute the decision—do it together.

- Evaluate the results; that is, identify what worked and what was not as valuable. Discuss it with your partner or team. Are the results what you had in mind?

- If needed, choose the second best option.

- Reevaluate—go back over the steps again.

Allowing yourself to cultivate confusion is a maturity development issue. When we were young, or when our addiction interfered with our maturity level, we felt we needed to know. Now that we're in recovery and growing in our maturity, we realize we do not "know it all" and that the group may be more powerful than just relying on ourselves. Different people in our lives mature at a different pace. Some of our colleagues, friends, lovers, or fellow recovering persons are ahead of us in their maturity, and we see and feel that by the comfort they have within their own skin. Others are still an open wound—one we tend to want to stay away from. We need both in our lives in order to learn what we need to learn and know what we have already learned. Leading with confusion helps us to develop a deeper knowledge of our own attitudes and feelings of knowledge and competency because we no longer feel we need to force our opinions on others. We can relax in our knowledge, be confused as to what the fabric of the other person means, and open our hearts to hear it.

Pairing that with the ability to stop our instinct to make a decision, any decision, helps us make a big switch from the limbic to the cortex. We are moving from an instinctual response to the deliberate action of collecting information, sharing it with others openly, learning of other ways to consider situations, and then critically thinking through each of those possible decisions and their likely outcomes. Just those steps alone cause the brain to fire in ways that were not part of our automatic, instinctual reactions. We are no longer "reacting"—we are proactive and acting in ways that are more mature and thoughtful. It takes a lot of practice and a release of the ego to get to this place. It means feeling the discomfort of not knowing, sharing, being vulnerable, and then acting in a way we are not used to acting. When we get to the place where we can do this, we know we are on a clear path to the cortex and a more hopeful life in which we are happier and more content with ourselves and those around us!

Mutual Decision Making for Change Exercise

Use this table to record the behavior you would both like to change, the new behavior you would both like to exhibit, the steps you will take to achieve this new behavior, and the date when you project the new behavior will be attained. If the outcome you were hoping for doesn't happen, reevaluate the steps you took and perhaps readjust your expectations.

Behavior to Be Changed	
New Behavior to Be Adopted	
Steps Required	
Date to Attain New Behavior	

Behavior to Be Changed	
New Behavior to Be Adopted	
Steps Required	
Date to Attain New Behavior	

Behavior to Be Changed	
New Behavior to Be Adopted	
Steps Required	
Date to Attain New Behavior	

BIG IDEA 5

Understand the Paradox of Control

We often hear the phrases "control junkie" or "control freak" to describe someone who repeatedly tries to control other people. This chapter begs the question: Is control by one person over others necessary, anywhere or anytime, in our lives? We need to explore how and why people feel the need to control others, the damage it does to relationships, and how two people can make the shift together to a collaborative style of relationship and conflict resolution.

True collaboration does not require control. This is the essence of Big Idea 5, Understand the Paradox of Control. Put simply, the harder I try to control you, the less successful I am at it—if control is seen as the degree to which I'm able to shape your thoughts and behavior to meet my needs. In working to control you, I lose control. I also lose your respect and your connection to me. In fact, I push you away and doom the relationship.

Here comes the paradox: When I do not work so hard to control you, and I share information and feelings with you in a sincere and open way, I have *more* influence on your thoughts and feelings. You are able to hear my words in a more meaningful way. Therefore, I have more ability to impact your life and the course of our relationship. It's not control. It's collaboration.

Adding Big Idea 5 to the Mix

The more we ponder and live the Big Ideas in this book, the more our relationships will change for the better. The ideas and exercises will no longer feel like something we are "trying" to do; they will feel natural and instinctive. As discussed previously, our first two instincts are to fight or flee when we feel threatened. A third response, to stand still in the moment, is one that must be developed if it's to be used effectively. Moving this third action to a more natural impulse means integrating these Big Ideas so they do become instinctual. If you stand still in the moment and consider what's going on in a difficult situation, you will eventually see which Big Idea will be most helpful. Most likely, the problem is your reaction to the conflict more than the issue of contention itself. Your challenge is to get your thoughts out of the old limbic grooves, the kind that produce impulsive behaviors, and into new cortex-based grooves and thought-based behaviors.

When you reflect on your past relationship experiences, try to see how these exercises could have changed the outcomes. You will get better at the process over time. For example, let's say you've successfully halted a heated discussion after a romantic partner hurled some hurtful words at you. You did not fling an accusatory statement back at your partner. Congratulations for knowing when to stand still in the moment! Now, consider whether you have enough information to be certain of the other person's intent.

The answer is likely no. Neither do you know whether you both share the same view of the real issue at hand. With these insights, you know you must go back to Big Idea 2, to determine intent, and Big Idea 3, to cultivate confusion, in the context of an open discussion with your partner.

In time, you will become more confident in determining the best ways to apply each Big Idea to current circumstances. Together they function as a powerful GPS tool to guide you through unfamiliar territory; your task is to keep them with you at all times, as you would any essential tool. Use these Big Ideas to bring resolution to situations that seem difficult or impossible. As you do, please understand that the integration of these ideas, tools, and exercises into your thoughts and behavior is a gradual process. You can't rein in your brain overnight!

The really good news is that adopting these ideas (including the often-threatening idea of giving up the need for control, which we cover in this chapter) will not set you apart from others, or put you at any social or professional disadvantage. To the contrary, these ideas and behavior changes are "attractors," not "detractors." As you apply them, you will feel and project more joy and peace and inner calm. People are attracted to that in others. They'll feel better about spending time with you and being in your presence. In contrast, if your stance is to compete with or control others, it will be reflected in what you say and how you say it to others.

The choice is really yours. Limbic- and cortex-driven thoughts and behaviors are two distinctly different ways of approaching life and relationships. You must decide what you want: Do you want to be right or be heard? Do you wish to be the know-it-all who "holds forth" in a one-way conversation in every situation? Or is it your desire to hear from others in a mutual give-and-take?

The Paradox of Control

- A paradox is a seemingly contradictory statement that may be true.
- The harder I try to control you, the less in control of you I am.
- The desire for control over one's environment and others is a basic human instinct.
- The common denominator of being human = "control junkie."
- The more we try to control others, the further we get from who we really are.
- Emotional manipulations to control others then become *who we are.*

How Control Junkies Manipulate Others

*The curious paradox is that when I accept myself
just as I am, then I can change.*

—CARL ROGERS

There are several "tried-and-true" manipulations people employ in their efforts to control the people close to them. Listed here are some common control mechanisms. The behaviors may sound familiar to you, from being on either the receiving or giving end. You might assume that control freaks would see themselves immediately in these descriptions. Interestingly, some start off totally unaware of their controlling nature and behaviors because their style is more covert (disguised or concealed) than overt (apparent).

Many, if not all, emotionally manipulative people have addictive behaviors or addictive personalities. This can lead us to become inordinately attached to all manner of things, both tangible and intangible. One such attachment is the control of others. Even a person whose primary flaw appears to be a tendency to remain in unhealthy relationships (with partners who publicly boss them around, for example) can still be a control junkie, albeit in secret.

Often these overly "nice" people believe they are the ones being manipulated, when in fact they operate on the assumption that their unconditional love for another can save (control) their partners and thus make them happy. They are addicted to the vision they carry of their partner's potential. In fact, these manipulators are held prisoner by their tendency to see diamonds in the rough they hope to "save." In addiction treatment terms, they are described as *codependent*. The love object for this type of person does not have to be a part-

Three Common Emotional Manipulations

- anger
- guilt
- withholding

ner. It could be a family member, a child, a best friend, or a colleague. The issue is not the "who." It is "what" they see in the other person. Their vision of this individual may not be shared by that person. The issue then becomes the codependent's desire to "save" and thereby control the other person.

Control and Addiction

Many of us with chronic relationship conflicts become dependent on some form of blame-based control behavior. These negative habits develop and follow a progressive path—not unlike addiction. Both share a similarity in our use of anger, guilt, and withholding, either overt or covert, and the abuse of alcohol and other substances. Both control and addiction give us an illusion of power. Another similarity is that we turn to these behaviors because of a desire to alter our mood or take the edge off an awkward emotional moment.

This subtle and sometimes not-so-subtle manipulation works fairly effectively in the early stages of relationships, especially during the Honeymoon stage of romance. In the beginning, neither manipulators nor their partners realize that this habit of self-alteration and pushing the other to change will become a problem later in the relationship. Denial kicks in. All of us are skilled at covering up our vulnerability and avoiding inconvenient truths. We get so good at it that we are no longer in touch with the pain and hurt hidden within us.

Persons with active substance use disorders rely on their substance of choice to help them cope and relax. It is less obvious (and yet equally true) that people with relationship problems become hopelessly dependent on some form of blame-based control (anger, guilt, and withholding). In both situations, these negative habits develop and follow a progressive path toward familiar addiction-type behaviors.

When We Realize We Don't Control Ourselves: Cynthia's Awakening Moment

My first go-round with recovery happened at age fifteen, after spending a month with my mother and feeling so sick in my body and so sick of the life of addiction we were all leading that I reached out for help and found it. During the next three years, recovery was a "full-on" process for me, living in my foster home and cleaning up all areas of my life. No more drugs, stealing, fighting, or skipping school. With the help of my foster parents, I started dealing with the emotional fallout from prior experiences of abuse and neglect.

While I was in college I considered using again. It started inconsequently (or so I thought) by taking NoDoz to stay awake studying. As time went on, my addiction caught up with me (really my brain), and there I was, using speed as if it were an old friend from long ago, wanting to catch up on old times! In my last year of college, I was about to start a field experience in an alcohol and drug information center, when the "big hit" came on New Year's Eve. "Party hardy" was on!

By the end of the night, I had consumed so much speed that my chest was aching—so much that I felt it was on the verge of bursting. I asked my husband to take me to the ER, but he became infuriated with me for using and said, "No way!" By the time we got to where we were staying, he was so disgusted he left me in the car. I crawled out onto the ground and lay there for a long time—the rapid beating of my heart hurting so bad, I cried out, only to realize that no one could hear me.

And then I said a prayer: "Lord, please allow me to live, and I promise if you do I will dedicate my life to helping people and families with alcoholism and drug addiction." I finally got it: I will repeat the legacy of my family of origin unless I change it. It starts with me—no matter what.

From that point, I could no longer pretend that this disease was not in my system. Any and all accountability to my recovery and the recovery of my family system was to begin with me. Thirty-some years later, my memory of that night is as vivid as it was the next morning.

Blame-Based Control Behaviors in Different Conflict Communication Styles

When conflict heats up, people use their primary (or secondary) conflict communication styles reflexively. Their goal is to stop the pain they are feeling as a result of the conflict, or at least reduce it, if only for a while. As discussed previously, this desire to control others manifests differently in different people. Some examples:

- Competitive people use their anger to get what they want through intimidation.

- Avoiders resort to offering the "cold shoulder" in order to get their point across and exercise control.

- Accommodators use guilt to manipulate the outcome of situations.

Another way to look at the desire to control others using blaming behaviors is by using the lens of the Twelve Steps, particularly Step One. It states that we are powerless to resist substances, and due to their hold over us, our lives have become unmanageable.

An addiction to control, like an addiction to substances, can be both physical and emotional in nature. Our bodies and minds are primed to take us down familiar paths, toward the impulsive habits we use to diminish pain and achieve control over someone or something. However, people who rely reflexively on anger, guilt, and withholding in emotional situations are destined to lose control over their lives and relationships, just as the addicted person does over alcohol and other drugs. Whereas chemically addicted persons will progressively use more and more in an unsuccessful effort to gain control over their unmanageable lives, control junkies have not yet learned that the more reactive (limbic) energy they invest in trying to manipulate another person, the less likely it is that they will get what they want. Nonetheless, they continue to try, and they succeed only in pushing other people away, often losing not only control over the outcome of a given conflict but also the relationship itself. Their sense of loss can be so great they finally "hit bottom" and seek another way to be in relationship with others. Alternatively, they may continue the same controlling behaviors with a new partner.

Adopting a Paradoxical Strategy

A fundamental concept that must be mastered if you are going to successfully adopt the paradox of control is this idea: The more I try to force you, the more you will fight me. In order to avoid the temptation to follow our instincts toward control, the application of a *paradoxical strategy* is essential. This means that somehow I have to empower you, my partner, to exercise your own free will and resist my efforts to control you so that our interaction does not degenerate along with the relationship.

By encouraging and allowing you to resist and hang on to your own free will, I have succeeded in making control a non-issue in our relationship. There will be less and less need for you to resist. Trust and mutual solution-focused problem solving can finally flow between us.

The ability to harness the energy you've previously wasted on attempts to control someone (or the energy you spent resisting another's control) and redirect it to a collaborative relationship is acquired over time. Rarely do persons come out of their family of origin with this ability intact. We are raised in families in which we learned some variation of "blame and control" in place of teamwork and mutual problem solving.

Many people have lost many relationships in their attempts to control another. Our minds do not like to be controlled; we like to think independently, even if we seem to be agreeing (Accommodator). As people in recovery, we remember the experience of believing we were in control of our disease, when we really were not. Now, we should consider whether controlling others is getting in the way of long-term and happy relationships . . . and is it worth it?

We are often taught to think about power in black-and-white terms; either I am in control and the powerful one, or you are in control and hold power over me. Power, in a typical limbic family system, is not shared. The key element few of us are taught is *mutual control* over a relationship or situation. Paradoxically, the power of mutual control is the power that this Big Idea helps unlock.

Accepting That "I Am Powerless over Control"

- Compare our desire to control others to our past attempts to control our use of alcohol and other drugs. Admit we are powerless over the need to control.
- Life becomes unmanageable the more we try to control others.
- The more reactive energy spent to manipulate others, the less likely we are to get what we want, which is a solution to conflict.
- The harder control is tried, the more others are pushed away—to the point of losing the relationship.

Exercises for Letting Go of Control

If you have ever listened to a progressive relaxation tape, you'll recall a calm, peaceful, and hypnotic voice telling you to lie on your back, find a comfortable position, and close your eyes. The voice then tells you to tense the muscles in your arms and legs, and clench your fists. After a pause, the voice tells you to relax those muscles. You're instructed to repeat this sequence several times. When the voice tells you to let go of your tension, you start to feel the warmth of blood as it returns to that portion of your body. The voice continues directing you to relax and feel the warmth moving into your fingertips and each part of your body.

What does this have to do with the paradox of control? It's simple. The voice guiding this relaxation method is tinkering with your resistance. In the exercises that follow, keep this idea in mind as you begin to play with your own resistance—to a life no longer ruled by control, blame, and shame.

Resistance Examples

Consider a husband and wife on a house-hunting trip talking about buying a specific house. In this example, the wife is pregnant with the couple's first child. The husband is working in a new job in which he doesn't yet feel secure.

> **Husband:** "No, I don't think so. We can't afford it. I think you're being hasty!"

> **Wife:** "Why not? We can afford what we want! Don't turn your back on me now—you promised!"

Stop. What if Wife said any of the following instead?

> **Wife:** "Okay, let's talk about the negatives. What are your reasons for hesitating?

> **Wife:** "Tell me what you're afraid of so I can understand what you're feeling."

> **Wife:** "Do you want to wait and see if the interest rates go down?"

> **Wife:** "I'm willing to put it off for a couple of months, and in the meantime, maybe we can keep looking so we get a feel for the market and what we both like."

What if she really listened to his fear and showed a willingness to do something to diminish it and, therefore, his resistance? Think how differently this exchange might go. Instead of her trying to force her partner out of his position, she invites him into a mutual exploration.

How and Why to Encourage Resistance

- The more I try to force you to do what I believe is good for you, the more you resist me.
- I must use a paradoxical strategy to encourage you to resist my control.
- This interaction leads to mutual problem solving.
- It allows us to build a mutual plan and implement it side by side.

What Happens When Resistance Is Denied

- Typical response—blaming others for not seeing our logic and the benefits of our position!
- Taking their resistance personally.
- Making assumptions.
- Throwing in rules.
- Throwing in the towel in the relationship.

What Happens When Resistance Is Addressed

- Listen carefully to the fear.
- Show sensitivity to the fear.
- Work with the fear.
- By doing these three things, we are able to move to a new level. Both parties can win. It leads to mutual problem solving, not just controlling or being controlled.

Sadly, it is more typical for one of the partners to get angry. Then blame is used, as one party doesn't see the logic or benefit of the solution pushed by the other party. They may take the partner's resistance personally. In the house-hunting example, the husband might feel his wife is "dumb" for suggesting the purchase of a house. If this is felt as criticism, the wife will feel compelled to make her husband's resistance go away. Depending on the conflict communication role the partners learned in their families of origin, they may feel challenged to the point of calling in a "rule" to force their position. For example, the husband's rule might be "As the man, I am the leader of this home, so what I say is going to stick." The wife's rule might be something like: "You promised me we'd buy our own house *before* we had children, and I want to cash in that promise now."

The Alternative to the Control-Resistance Cycle

A win-win solution is built on one partner encouraging the other to express his or her fear and resistance and the two thoroughly exploring these feelings together. It is based on the premise that all questions and concerns are valid. In the husband and wife example, it is vital that the wife not view her husband as a case of "my will versus your will."

Each party needs to hear what the other has to say. If they do, this dynamic will change their decision and the outcome of their conflict. This, in fact, may not be the best time to purchase a house. If the wife is wrong and pushes her husband past his comfort zone in order to get her way, then they both lose! The only win-win in this process is for both parties to get all the information on the table. A process needs to be established that promotes both partners' getting their needs met, and avoids viewing any resistance from their parter on a personal level. For the outcome to be worthwhile for both parties, they must adopt an attitude of mutual responsibility for whatever issue is on the table. In other words, it's not "my problem," or "your problem." It's "our problem" to solve together.

In order to work with resistance in a healthy way, we begin with thinking through, together, all the options to the issue we are facing. Discussing the options together gives us the opportunity to learn more about the thought process of each other and what is important to each person. In deciding on an option, we now become accountable for that decision as a *we* and not just a *me* decision. We now own mutual accountability and responsibility. There is no need to blame down the road should the decision not turn out as hoped. This builds internal self-control by recognizing that the decision was mutual and there is no need to blame or now control the other person because of the outcome of the decision.

What is helpful in this process is to write down your agreement and the next ideas or steps should the decision not meet expectations. Then, if needed, go back to that agreement and discuss the plan and its backup ideas. Should the couple decide at this point that the whole plan needs to be reviewed and retooled, it may be done by looking at the options together again and making a mutual choice. The idea is to not get into a position where only one person is making decisions, especially life-changing decisions. When only one person is responsible for big decisions, they give the other permission to blame, shame, and control when it does not turn out as planned.

In the Honeymoon stage, we are not looking to control the other person; we are just happy to be with the person. It is in the later stages of a relationship that we work to control the other. Once you have agreed within yourself not to push for control, it allows both of you to feel those excited feelings from the Honeymoon stage. Each person can be more free to love and express affection, without waiting for the shoe of control to drop and stop the loving flow of the relationship.

Learning Our Parents' Lessons

Most people in recovery had parents who were still living "under the influence" of parent-child struggles from their own childhoods. One parent may have been the over-responsible one, while the other played the role of the under-responsible one in the relationship. Almost universally, one party in a relationship where addiction is present is stuck in a chronic juvenile-like state of irresponsibility. This is true of families where alcoholism, workaholism (unavailability to the family), or addiction to gambling, shopping, eating, controlling others, or sex are present. The power and control inequities embedded in these adult relationships can create wall-to-wall "gridlock" in terms of settling family conflicts. We may have reached adulthood without witnessing a single experience that illuminated what healthy adult-to-adult interactions look like. Our view of what is "normal" was tainted, and we are just awakening to that realization.

We can obtain insight into what we do to contribute to inequality in our own relationships and families by looking again at what we learned from the Thomas-Kilmann conflict styles. We tend to learn reactive styles (accommodating, avoiding, and competing) from our parents or caretakers. If adult Accommodators and Avoiders take on an over-responsible, permissive parental role with their partners, they probably grew up identifying with someone who did more than his or her fair share to keep the peace in the family, or stayed out of harm's way. The children of such people grow up and instinctively clean up everyone else's messes. They over-control themselves, putting them at higher risk for depression and anxiety disorders.

When children identify with an over-responsible parent who competed, they grow up witnessing the Competer seize power because of what they saw as incompetence or insubordination from other family members. When such children become adults, they

Competers who become over-responsible

- seize control because they think others are incompetent
- develop insubordinate behaviors
- have a strong need to control
- become angrier over time
- have a need to punish
- have a tendency to undermine healthy horizontal interactions

Accommodators and Avoiders tend to

- develop the tendency to be over-responsible
- become permissive as a parent or significant other since they don't want to make waves
- identify with those who do "more than their fair share" in a relationship
- work to keep the peace or stay out of harm's way
- clean up everybody's messes
- overly control themselves
- have a need to rescue
- become depressed or anxious

internalize the traits of the parent who over-controlled others and become angrier as time goes by.

By absorbing the patterns of over-responsible parents, whether they used a permissive or disciplinarian approach, all three of the reactive styles will likely take on belief systems tainted by the need to either rescue or punish others they are close to. Subsequently, they bring to their adult-to-adult relationships a built-in tendency to undermine healthy interactions between equals.

At the other end of the continuum, when Accommodators and Avoiders identify with an under-responsible parent, they adopt the pattern of being a "big kid." They make hollow promises, procrastinating and rarely following through on the commitments they make. Under-responsible people who turn out to be Competers were taking mental notes as a parent raged on about their right to be self-indulgent and pitched fits when other members of the family didn't do as they wanted. In any of these gridlock-producing control struggles, power is just as likely to end up in the hands of someone who is acting under-responsibly as someone acting over-responsibly. When this is the case, the family's energies are continually focused on the needs of the "infant" in the household.

Regardless of which type of parental role we were most influenced by growing up, and what we display as adults, the outcome in most of our adult-to-adult relationships is the same—a standoff! We are most likely to pick someone whose reactive style feels comfortable, and that is usually the opposite style to our own.

This means that over-responsible people frequently pair up with under-responsible partners. The two lock horns, just like their moms and dads did, over issues such as paying bills or disciplining the kids. Over time, these couples place more and more blame on each other for their individual and collective woes. They're in a constant struggle for control. They do not stop to figure out how to work together in mutual problem-solving solutions as two responsible adults might. Nobody taught them how.

Take a fresh look at your adult-to-adult relationships. Think about and write down any hidden parent-child dynamics from your childhood that contribute to a state of perpetual gridlock in your present-day household.

One way to think about this is to see relationships as being either vertical or horizontal. In a vertical structure, someone is on top and in control and someone is on the bottom and being controlled. This causes the person on top to be over-responsible, feeling the need to lead the way. The person on the bottom of the structure can feel under-responsible and is relieved at not having to lead or take responsibility for the relationship. People who live in the reactive styles (accommodate, avoid, compete) find it more natural to live in a vertical relationship. The Competer or Accommodator sits at the top being over-responsible while the Avoider is comfortable being under-responsible at the bottom. Blame and shame are part of the pieces that hold this structure together. There is an unspoken acceptance that someone will be blamed. Energy is spent blaming rather than reviewing options and coming to a new solution.

In order to mature and grow to a healthier style, the horizontal structure is preferred. This structure offers mutual control, mutual accountability, and responsibility. Decision making and problem solving are shared, and if something goes wrong, accountability to solve and correct it is mutual. Blame and shame are not pieces of the behavior holding this structure together. There is a spoken acceptance that the couple or team will put their energy into reviewing the issues behind a decision that is not working and come to new solutions.

The following is an illustration of how these structures appear:

Figure 3. Horizontal/Vertical Relationship Structure

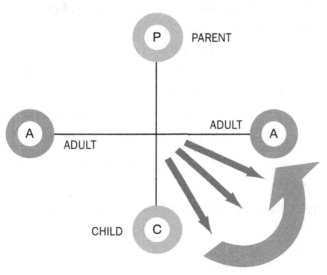

The arrows show that by moving away from the vertical relationship, we gradually tilt the balance closer to a horizontal one. Consider your past and current relationships. What patterns are most familiar to you? Is this the pattern you want to continue? Are there changes to your relationship structures you would like to make and, if so, in what situations (romantic partner, friends, family, work)?

Exercises to Help You Change Your Brain and Patterns

Please find the Paradox of Control exercise near the end of this chapter. In this exercise you will do the following:

- List the areas you try to control in work and personal relationships.
- Describe the resistance you receive in return from others.
- Describe what that resistance costs you in those relationships.
- Record what you believe you would gain if you let go of the control and shared it with the other people in your life.

Please refer to the Impulse Control exercise at the end of this chapter. In this exercise you will select which conflict style is your primary style. The first contract example is for people scoring highest in *compete*. The second contract example is for people scoring highest in *avoid* or *accommodate*. On the blank Impulse Control Contract, please do the following:

- Write the behavior(s) you need to take responsibility for.
- Write the impulse control steps you will follow.
- Write the consequences you will accept if you do not follow through.
- Sign it. Refer to it often and remind your brain how you want to be.

Once you have completed your list of behaviors you are to take responsibility for (on the Impulse Control Contract), decide what needs to change in order to improve your relationship. What will happen to your relationship if nothing changes? We all must decide what it's worth to us—to change or to remain the same. It is our life to take back from our instinctual self. We do not have to be bonded to our "old ways." We all have the ability to create new behaviors and approaches to changing our need to control others.

Paradox of Control Exercise

Use the following table to list the areas you try to control in your work and personal relationships. Describe the type of resistance you get in return from others. Describe what this resistance costs you. Record what you believe you would gain if you let go of that control and shared it with the other people in your life.

	In Work Relationships	In Personal Relationships
I try to control the following areas of my life:		
In return, I get the following resistance from others:		
This resistance costs me the following:		
If I let go of the control and shared it with the other people in my life, I believe I would gain the following:		

Impulse Control Contracts

On the following pages, you will find two Impulse Control Contracts. The first one is an example that shows someone who scores highest in *compete*. Competers tend to overreact in emotional moments and say mean things. The second example shows a person who scores highest in *avoid* or *accommodate*. Avoiders and accommodators need to hold themselves more accountable for putting things off, minimizing, or making hollow promises.

A blank Impulse Control Contract has been provided for you to complete. The spirit of this process is the promotion of more self-control (or impulse control). The completed contract will spell out a price you agree to pay if you fail to do your fair share of promoting healthier, horizontal adult-to-adult relationships.

Behaviors to take responsibility for:

- getting too angry, too fast
- being too intense
- holding anger for a long time
- saying "sorry" too quickly
- minimizing or avoiding

Impulse control steps to follow:

- repeat my mantra
- take a time out (e.g., go for a walk)
- dig deeper and get more information
- decide what you need to take responsibility to change

Consequences I will accept:

- participate in an individual or family session
- seek spiritual help
- share the problem with a friend and get his or her feedback
- take time out for yourself
- dig deeper into your need to do the behavior you need to change

Impulse Control Contract Example for Competers

The behavior I need to take responsibility for:

Getting angry and saying mean things.

The impulse control steps I will follow:

Set an egg timer for two minutes to allow time to blow off steam.

Ask myself why I have a need to behave in this manner. Where is this behavior familiar to me?

The consequences I will accept for lack of follow through:

Clean the bathroom, including the toilet bowl.

Listen to my significant other explain to me how my behavior offends her.

Signed:

Chuck

Impulse Control Contract Example for Avoiders or Accommodators

The behavior I need to take responsibility for:

Putting things off—not following through within a specified period of time.

Putting my real feelings off—not speaking to my needs.

The impulse control steps I will follow:

Even if I innocently forget, I agree to pay a price for not holding myself more accountable.

Allow myself to change my impulse to avoid conflict by walking into the situation by explaining my feelings in a collaborative manner.

The consequences I will accept for lack of follow through:

1. *Cook a candlelight dinner for two OR*
2. *Watch the kids while my partner takes time for himself.*
3. *Dig deeper into my avoiding behavior—where is this behavior familiar to me?*

Signed:

Cindy

Impulse Control Contract

The behavior I need to take responsibility for:

_____

_____

_____

_____

The impulse control steps I will follow:

_____

_____

_____

_____

The consequences I will accept for lack of follow through:

_____

_____

_____

_____

Signed:

_____

BIG IDEA 6

Dismantle the Wall of Misunderstanding

Every one of us is convinced that we—not the other person in conflict with us—know *the Truth* . . . with a capital "T." We have a need to "know," or at least be seen as knowing. Uncertainty is something we instinctually avoid—all of us, as a species. In terms of mankind's early survival, those who knew where to find food or how to defend against a predator became the leaders of their people. Knowledge becomes power over others. Fast-forward 350,000 years and, on an instinctual level, not all that much has changed for modern man.

When we think we know something the other person doesn't, or if things are not going the way we want them to go in a conflict, we often feel compelled to either interrupt the conversation or in some way point out an error in the other's reasoning. Even though modern humans live in a world of much greater complexity, if we don't catch ourselves and our mammalian limbic systems before it's too late, we still see reality in black-or-white terms. This worldview leaves little room for a gray area, let alone the diversity of twenty-first-century ideas!

Consider this idea: In interpersonal communication, there is always more than one truth.

The intensity with which we feel we are right (and the other person is wrong) in a conflict stems in part from the moment of peak emotional impact. Our emotional pain has amplified and fixed the event in our minds. We are momentarily unable to hear any other explanation than our own. Simply remembering this fact about human nature is a good first step. Big Idea 6, Dismantle the Wall of Misunderstanding, encourages us to loosen our grip on being "right" or "correct" and reopen our minds to seeing something other than a one-dimensional interpretation—our view and ours alone.

In the end, we will be forced to choose: Do we want to be right (all the time) or happy? Clinging to a single-capital-"T" Truth often means winning the battle and losing the war. When winning at any cost, or making others pay, is our primary goal, there will be no peace in our relationship. If you insist on using this approach, "happily ever after" will be an impossibility.

Misunderstanding Because of Wanting to Be Right

Applying Big Idea 6 is more difficult for Competers than those using other conflict styles or reactive categories (Accommodators and Avoiders). If you're a Competer, question whether your loved ones may be living in secret fear of your response to tense moments or situations that are uncomfortable or painful for you. Competers feel the need to be right because it is attached with status, power, and competence. Competers create a wall by working to hide their fear of not being competent or knowledgeable. This creates a wall that hides Competers from their fear of vulnerability. It also creates a wall between them and their loved ones or colleagues. The loved ones don't understand what is happening; they just feel the resentment and force of the Competer.

This does not let the Accommodators and Avoiders off the

hook. Often, they simply take longer before they too explode. Eventually, Accommodators and Avoiders will turn against others or themselves! There is little understanding that Accommodators do not always feel cheerful and helpful, so when the explosion finally occurs, others around them are in shock. Avoiders have been quiet and hidden, so when they finally explode, others are also not expecting it and are in shock.

Your explosive reactions may have everyone running for cover. Family members, friends, coworkers, and romantic partners are going to try to soften the blows (by withholding information) and maybe even claim ignorance rather than face your reactions. Consider whether your conflict style has your family or colleagues walking on eggshells. Before you start passing out judgments or damaging remarks (e.g., you're lying, you don't know anything, what the heck are you talking about) about your significant others or colleagues, look deeper into the mirror and try to see an underlying truth about yourself. It just may be people are afraid of telling you what is actually happening as a result of your behavior.

With Big Idea 6, it's no longer necessary to remain stuck in the black-and-white world of who's right or wrong. When you feel yourself about to go down the road of "my way or the highway," ask yourself, *Would I rather be right or happy?* Make this question your personal mantra. Say it often enough and you will eventually

---

Capital "T" Truth

- The stronger the tendency to compete, the more likely Competers will see themselves as "experts" on what is right and what is wrong.

- Accommodators and Avoiders wed themselves to their own personal Truth and often hide it from themselves or others until they blow up.

- Big Idea 6 encourages us to go beyond the one-dimensional interpretation of our view and our view alone.

see that, in a healthy relationship, there can be a *mutual truth,* a view of the way things are to which both partners contribute equally. You will learn a way of interpreting events where no one has to be called a liar or a fool.

Healthy Relationships Allow Do-Overs

When you are in a disagreement, always make room for the option to start over and say what each partner means to say. What the other person understood from your words or actions might not have the remotest connection to what you were trying to get across. It is always helpful to separate yourself from your first reading of the conflict. Take time in the middle of any discussion of the facts to speculate how your differing opinions might simply be different views of the same exact thing. Check it out. Work to conduct a discussion like two well-intentioned adults, rather than as a victim and a perpetrator.

These ideas apply to every relationship, not just your closest ones. When we get stuck in "our Truth" at home or at the office, we create a wall of anger or resentment with others that is difficult to tear down. This wall may be displayed in anger, resentment, hurt, or avoidance. The wall is there, in any case. No one wins or moves forward with a wall in the way. After letting any anger subside, think about your part in the conversation with your partner as a four-step process:

1. Repeat what you believe you said.

2. Find out what the other person heard you say.

3. Agree that a misunderstanding between you is creating a wall.

4. Agree to tear down the wall, together.

At this point you can think about what you missed the first time around, and perhaps why you missed it. And then start the conversation over.

What Do-Overs Allow

- Both parties to start over and say what they meant to say in the way they meant to say it.
- Both parties to acknowledge they may have heard something incorrectly.
- Both parties to divorce themselves from their first reading of the conflict.
- Both parties to recognize they may have different opinions that are essentially saying the same thing.
- Both parties to see how misunderstanding creates a wall between them.
- Both parties to agree to tear down the wall together.

Tearing down the wall that both of you built is the ultimate goal. Understanding how the wall was built—who said what, how it was perceived, what words were misunderstood, and which non-verbal communications and projections of feelings contributed to the wall—is essential if you are going to successfully dismantle it.

When we take the time to learn how what we've said is causing confusion, we can remove one layer of bricks from the wall. When we're able to discuss with the other person how we feel and what we would like to feel instead, then he or she has the tools to help us tear down the rest of the wall. We can then agree that no one is at fault. Remember, no one likes to be "at fault." Letting go of the need to blame or shame keeps the wall from reappearing. Allowing for others to save face and receive the benefit of "misunderstanding" gives both parties the opportunity to begin again on equal footing.

Goal: Tearing Down the Wall

Tools

- understanding how the wall got there
- understanding how the wall was built over time
- recognizing the misunderstandings each person has
- learning how the misunderstanding is causing the other person to feel
- discussing how you feel
- discussing how you both would like to feel instead, and building agreement in a healthy manner
- agreeing no one is at fault—it is a true misunderstanding
- together—tear down the wall!

Using Fear as Your Guide

Big Idea 4, Cultivate Confusion, suggests that confusion should be our first response when faced with conflict. The next important emotion to identify in ourselves is fear. As cool and macho as it might be to act tough and never let other people see us sweat, I highly recommend that you go right ahead and sweat. (You're going to anyway!) And the more publicly we can do it, the better. Covering up our vulnerability will come back to haunt us every time.

Normally, fear is associated with retreat-and-defeat or attack-and-defend. The more frightened we become, the less and less likely we are to think creatively about solving problems. However, if we consciously lead with our fear, we will be able to inch into conflicts with extreme delicacy. Instead of our fight-or-flight, blame-based impulses, which inevitably get in the way of more effective strategies, we can cautiously open sensitive subjects without pointing fingers.

How to Lead with Your Fear

Try saying these sentences out loud and check in with your body to see how you feel:

- "I'm afraid of saying anything about this for fear of hurting your feelings. Our relationship is too important, though, for me to remain silent. I'm worried about your drinking more regularly. Are you?"

- "My fear is that your unwillingness to talk with me is an indication that you just don't want me around. Is that accurate?"

Putting our toe in the water to test the temperature before we dive in makes sense. In moments when we feel most vulnerable, we're tempted to skip this systematic approach of information gathering. We'd rather make a big splash by making accusations or cover up by saying nothing or acting like nothing's wrong. Taking the risk of sharing what we're afraid of is a most courageous and practical act. We express our own concerns while gathering information in a nonconfrontational way.

Fear Is a Two-Way Street

We must learn to trust the people close to us enough to talk unflinchingly about our vulnerability and ask for feedback. Tearing down the barriers of cocksureness, niceness, graciousness, or cool aloofness that we normally hide behind allows us to show our vulnerability. In the face of painful circumstances, we can let our fear guide us like a light through the darkness. By doing so, we will discover a new way of being with one another.

Medical practitioners use this same methodical approach in working with patients who are presenting symptoms. A physician, attempting to diagnose an illness, performs tests to help rule out some of the more radical explanations behind the patient's issues. Finding out whether a patient's condition is life threatening is a step-by-step process of elimination. Only after a correct diagnosis and appropriate treatment will the patient recover.

A patient experiencing these same symptoms without the benefit of a doctor's diagnostic tests or expertise might blow the situation out of proportion. Left to sketch in the details of the "big picture" without sufficient information, a patient is liable to jump to the conclusions. How often have we had an upset stomach or headache and immediately thought "cancer"?

We do the same projecting in a relationship conflict when fear keeps us from sharing our truth. We project this fear on the other person, ensuring that the outcome of the disagreement will be more painful, hurtful, or horrible than it needs to be. Verbalizing our fears allows both parties to eliminate the incorrect issues and focus on the correct ones. It is better to know "what is" than to guess, risk being wrong, and miss the opportunity to work on solving the real problem together. If you don't work it—it will work you!

If your fear wants you to believe that something another person did or said means he or she no longer cares about you, don't go there! And don't hide your fear or let it fester and distort your view. Go public with what worries you. Don't assume the other person "shoulda, coulda, woulda" anticipated how you were going to feel. Accidental misunderstandings in relationships are a given. The chances are more likely that your worst fears are overblown. Don't interpret what a significant other feels or wants until you have verified that this is what the person meant.

Instead of guessing what our partner means, we must get him or her to help us rule in or rule out the scarier and more radical interpretations of what just happened. This is a more valuable way of harnessing our fears and worries. We can turn fear from a liability into an asset if we don't get ahead of ourselves. By regularly seeking the other person's input, we can cautiously proceed with the diagnosis. Let the other person fill in the blanks for us.

Sensitivity Spots and Stress Cycles

Stress in relationships runs in cycles. A stressful situation can grow into a full-blown relationship burnout or blowup if not checked and discussed by both partners early on in the cycle. Keep in touch with this concept as you work through your relationship "sensitivity spots." They are the very same areas that will trigger your cycle of stress.

Cycle of Stress

- We start with the "sensitivity spot."
- The sensitivity spot creates stress.
- We hold on to the stress and fear.
- We don't discuss it with our partner, which strengthens the "sensitivity spot," making it more likely to come up later.

How to Reverse Stress

- Start with the "sensitivity spot."
- Bring it out in the light to create awareness.
- Realize that the worst that could happen is already in our thought process.
- Recognize that the worst is not likely to happen.
- Recognize that if it did happen, it most likely would have happened anyway. Refuse to be held hostage by our fears.
- Discuss our fears with our partner.
- Come to agreements about the "sensitivity spot."
- Implement new behaviors to address it in the future.

At the beginning of a stress cycle, we hold on to our fear and we resist discussing it. As a result, the stress only increases. In our thought process we are already holding tight to a picture of the worst thing that could happen—even though it probably won't happen. And even if it did happen, it would have happened with or without our fear and increasing stress. It's better to learn the truth now than continue in a hurtful relationship, just waiting for it to end or blow up.

Inventory Your Fears

In recovery, we learn to make a moral inventory of ourselves—our resentments, our character defects, and our past harms. In my own recovery, I have found it helpful to list my fears and the behaviors that I reverted to in the past. Please take a few moments to jot down your worst fears. Consider how your fears affect your reactions when you communicate with others in conflicts, as well as in neutral situations. Consider how you can identify and use your feelings of fear to discuss sensitive subjects with people to whom you are close, especially feelings that have frequently resulted in accidental collisions and misunderstandings.

For example, let's suppose your worst fear is being left or abandoned. When you experience this fear, it causes you to become more clingy and controlling toward another person. To describe this fear to the person you are close to, you might say:

"My fear is that you will leave me if I tell you how I really feel."

Then, describe how you do *not* want your behavior to change when you are feeling that fear. For example:

"I don't want to get more clingy and controlling in order to feel better, so I would like instead to know if you're committed to working out the misunderstandings that happen in our relationship as a result of my fear."

This creates an agreement that feeds into the Four Fabulous Agreements (financial, physical, emotional/psychological/social, spiritual), adding to your own sense of peace and calm in the relationship—and relaxing both your fear and feelings of stress around it.

When these types of "sensitivities" from past issues, hurts, fears, and disappointments come into our lives, our inner self causes an "amplifier effect." This amplification causes us to hear and react to certain situations in a harsher or more extreme manner than we otherwise would. Below is a table that can help you identify your "sensitivity spot" and that of someone else.

Table 2. The Amplifier Effect

Truth #1	What I meant to say
Truth #2	What I say
Truth #3	What you hear
Truth #4	How it makes you feel

Table 3. Example of the Amplifier Effect

Truth #1	What I meant to say	I'm going to the grocery store.
Truth #2	What I say	I guess I'll go to the grocery store.
Truth #3	What you hear	I don't really want to go to the grocery store.
Truth #4	How it makes you feel	Annoyed that "I" cannot do a simple task without whining.

The purpose of this exercise is to help us dig deeper into a simple verbal exchange in order to get to the truth about what we're trying to communicate.

Thinking back to Big Idea 4, Cultivate Confusion, this idea of amplifier effects tied to sensitivity spots also looms large when we discuss our partner's expressed fear, for example, a fear of abandonment. Your partner may make what appears to be a contradictory statement, such as declaring that he or she plans to leave the relationship. Try staying with that confusion by saying:

"I heard you say earlier that your fear of abandonment causes you to become clingy and controlling. What I am hearing from you now is that you're ready to run away. I am confused; what's causing this new behavior?"

If the person is an Avoider, it may be easier for him or her to leave the relationship rather than work through the issue. It takes nurturing and reassuring on the partner's part to point out the confusing behavior, and it takes courage for the fearful partner to remain in the conversation and work to find a solution other than running away.

When we understand our style of conflict, we will be able to discern the parallels between that style and our past pain, and how this linkage results in behaviors that undermine healthy relationships. Staying in the relationship and standing still in the moment of confusion is essential to figuring out our best course of action. Reminding ourselves that we want to truly understand the other person and work toward a win-win is also helpful in these situations.

As just discussed, our fears can actually guide us to the areas that we need to work on in order to become healthier in relationships. So rather than viewing our fears as shameful problems, we can think of them as blessings to guide us to the resolutions that will bring us happiness. These fears become critical information we need in order to see the work we have to do and the areas we need to solve.

Amplifier Effect

- Our past issues, fears, hurts, and disappointments amplify how we see, hear, and perceive things.

- Understand the fears that work as amplifier effects in your life.

- Remind yourself of Big Idea 4, Cultivate Confusion, to work through the tough spots.

- View fears as a blessing—knowing them can guide you, like a light, to the work you have yet to do.

- Inch your way into the conflict with delicacy.

- Allow the conversation to help you both learn more and work through your issues.

Tying In the Brain

This may also be a good time to remind ourselves of using the cortex words (see appendix B) as our own level of fear, anger, or passion pushes into our limbic system. Look for that level rising and ask yourself, "Am I wanting to build the relationship up, keep it level, or tear it down?" If the issue is worth tearing the relationship down over, remind yourself of how bad you feel when limbic words and behaviors are used on you.

Write the cortex words on a sticky note, sheet of paper, or your hand and practice saying them. Repeating them often will lead to practicing different actions and changing your brain. You are in charge of your brain, and the more you "work it" versus its "working you," the happier and healthier you and your loved ones will be. You will become the guiding light.

Fear Exercise

1. List your worst fears and the behaviors you demonstrate when you experience them:

Fear	Behavior
1.	1.
2.	2.
3.	3.
4.	4.
5.	5.

2. Review Big Idea 6, Dismantle the Wall of Misunderstanding, and describe how you can discuss sensitive subjects with the people you're close to. For example, suppose your worst fear is being left or abandoned. When you experience this fear, you become more clingy and controlling.

3. Create a sentence using your fear: *"My fear is that you'll leave me if I tell you how I really feel."*

_____

_____

_____

_____

_____

4. Describe how you do *not* want your behavior to change when you are feeling that fear: *"I do not want to get more clingy and controlling in order to feel better. What I would like instead is to know if you are committed to working out the misunderstandings that happen in our relationship as a result of my fear."*

_____

_____

_____

_____

_____

BIG IDEA 7

Create a Blameless
Relationship with Yourself

We have discussed several Big Ideas to help us stop using impulsive behaviors and start using new tools in order to live and work more thoughtfully and peacefully with others.

- In the chapter on Big Idea 5, we focused on the paradox of control. We looked at strategies for working creatively with our desire to control other people and with our reaction to their resistance.

- In the previous chapter on Big Idea 6, I described the importance of dismantling the wall of misunderstanding between you and another by recognizing sensitivity spots from the past and working with the stress cycle in relationships. We ended that chapter with new ways to approach and sustain conversations with another person while we experience conflict.

Throughout this book, we've returned to one central question as our guide: *Will what I'm about to say, and the way I'm going to say it, build the relationship up, keep it level, or tear it down?*

Big Idea 7, Create a Blameless Relationship with Yourself, is a precondition for having a blameless relationship with a partner. This Big Idea depends on how carefully you've considered two questions covered in earlier chapters:

1. How does the role you played in your family continue to play a part in your style of conflict in adult relationships?

2. What types of difficulties in your relationships trigger you to revert to a limbic response learned in your family?

These questions point to an essential issue each of us must grapple with as we navigate our present-day relationships: To see how the emotional baggage we still carry from past unhealthy relationships interferes with our best efforts to leave old ways behind and find new pathways away from impulsivity.

To go deeper into the issue of the baggage we carry, we'll work with the list of fears compiled in the previous chapter. Our goal is to be more productive in conversations with partners, especially when we experience conflict, by getting the old baggage out of our way.

Developing New Lifelong Tools

One of the most valuable tools we've worked with thus far is the use of a mantra. This tool slows down the limbic processes of our brains and allows us to move into the cortex for help in problem solving. Keep that tool in mind as we move through this work on blameless relationships. By remembering that this is a process, we give ourselves permission to change old habits based on shame and blame. We must also forget about how long it may take to feel "normal." The changes of thought and behavior we're learning may not feel fully comfortable until our brains acclimate and adjust. Then the new ways will feel more "normal," while the old, limbic responses begin to feel distinctly wrong or unnatural. This is a gradual process.

The first six Big Ideas introduced you to techniques, skills, and tools to draw the other person into a conversation that is essentially a process of *we* decision making. As you practiced these ideas and exercises, you probably discovered that *we* also means *you*. In fact, the most productive and proactive place to begin this change is with *you*.

Looking inside ourselves and figuring out how to develop a blameless relationship with ourselves is like peeling back the layers of an onion. An issue we discover at our outer layer of exploration may require further work deep inside to determine its true meaning. On the surface, what makes us uniquely human is that we all have a variety of *selves*. In and among these selves, we can be in a near-constant, albeit silent, debate about what we should do and how we feel. Frequent topics for this "self-talk" include "should I stay married/get divorced, drink/not drink, be brave/play it safe, push harder/stand back a little." It goes on and on.

Examining our silent self-talk helps us see directly into our relationship with ourselves. If we record this debate and review it, we can begin to see clearly the effects of how we were raised. With thoughtful study, we can learn how to cut the invisible apron strings that bind us to old patterns and behaviors that limit emotional functioning in the present.

These patterns and behaviors are usually learned in our families of origin. In toxic families, they are more forcefully projected onto individual family members and adhered to in the family system. In such families, the playing out of respective roles takes on a more compulsive nature. These roles are needed in order for the family to function, as well as to hide what is happening in the family, such as addiction, anger, and control. In healthier families, individuals are allowed to change, work through issues, and grow strong. Parents have a clear role and children are allowed to be children, with healthy boundaries between them.

Family Roles: Which Were You?

The roles discussed here may be familiar to you from previous readings or presentations. They are a fairly well-known set of roles developed by Sharon Wegscheider-Cruse, an educator, speaker, and author who studies family dynamics and psychology. Please review them in the context of conflict styles and other information shared thus far. See how they take on a clearer picture when matched with your conflict styles. Challenge yourself to understand how these patterns and roles occurred in your family of origin.

Creating a Blameless Relationship with Yourself

- Creating a blameless relationship with yourself happens when you approach the process in stages, as if you are peeling back the layers of an onion.
- Examining your self-talk helps you to see directly into your relationship with yourself.
- Recording these conversations may help you see the effects of being raised in your family of origin.
- You can learn to cut the invisible apron strings that bind you to old patterns and behaviors.

Hero

The Hero child is often (although not always) the first-born. Often, there are more pictures, videos, and memorabilia of the first child than of any of the other children, partly because of the novelty of being the first child, and partly because of time, energy, and financial and emotional constraints. This child often receives the best of toys, clothes, family heirlooms, and such. The parents' actions are not totally conscious; they act simply because this is the first child.

If you are not the first child in your family, and you have seen the Hero role played out toward a sibling, it is difficult not to blame the first child for being "special" or the favorite. Consider that this first child did not choose this role—it was placed upon him or her. Consider also that this "specialness" comes with a price.

Much is expected from first children. They are taught to be the "image holders" of the family. This child identifies with doing the "right thing." This is the child who works hard to do well at school, takes care of issues at home, and may step in to help dissolve conflict—regardless of age. This is the child who looks after others—often in a compulsive manner. This is also the child who is not allowed to fail. First children must do well—for the sake of the family image. In the extreme, these dynamics become a toxic situation for all involved in the family system.

In toxic families, the Hero is important because the other family members can point to him or her and say to themselves and the world that all is well; it must be, because look at how well the family Hero is doing. No one is looking behind the mask of the Hero, who does not have a choice other than to feign perfection.

This person may grow up to be a Competer, feeling compelled to win at all costs while faking well-being. Sometimes this person will grow up to be an Accommodator, wanting everything and everyone to be taken care of. However, none of these traits and tendencies develops 100 percent in any one person. The role of Hero describes a set of tendencies and aspirations. This person is afraid not to know what to do in a situation and may throw out an answer just to have one. Throughout life, these persons may work to always look good, do good, and be seen as good. They are conflicted in that they do not believe they have the right to be their own person and learn who they really are.

In toxic families, the real difference is the degree to which individuals live out the role they're given early in life. In a healthy family system, on the other hand, each person may occupy a role temporarily or only in specific situations. It's like wearing one hat for a while, then trading it for another.

In toxic family systems, each person is required (often with nonverbal cues) to be exactly who and what the family has designated them to be. The family members feel safe when they know who "wears" what role, and they only change or trade a role if someone leaves or enters the family system. Toxicity, and therefore dysfunction, occurs because the children are not allowed to try on different styles and learn how those styles work in different settings, nor are they allowed to grow up being children in their own developmental process.

The Hero Child

- Often the first-born (not always)
- Identifies with doing the "right" thing
- Works hard, takes care of things in the family
- May step in to sort out conflict
- Looks after others—in a compulsive manner
- Toxicity or dysfunction is triggered when the child is compelled by self or others to remain in this role

The Hero child offers the family:

- The feeling that all is well—look at this great child
- Image control—fake perfection
- Parental stability
- Social norms are met
- Ability to "fit in" with other families

Scapegoat

The second common role in family systems is that of Scapegoat. This child cannot compete with the family Hero, as that role is already taken. This is the child who often becomes identified as the "problem child" in some way. Often the entire family's dysfunction or toxicity is projected onto this child, allowing the family to avoid any larger issue by hiding its toxicity in this child.

The role of this child is to take on the blame and shame of the family. As this child grows, he or she begins to see the family dysfunction for what it is, and may try to point this out to other family members. Most often, no one wants to hear or believe it. The members in a toxic family system are in place and do not want to hear what they could do to change it, to make more sense of it, or to make it more healthy. The Scapegoat grows up feeling rejected. Because of rejection, this person may decide that it's better to live to fight another day and thus become an Avoider. Again, this doesn't happen 100 percent of the time . . . it is more a tendency.

The Scapegoat child most likely shoulders the family blame and is often the first one to leave the family system. This often is the child who uses drugs and alcohol early, may become sexually involved early, and may become pregnant or cause a pregnancy in order to "have permission" to leave the family. He or she may end up in the justice system and institutions, finding yet another way to escape the family. Because of the observed difficulties in which these children become involved, they are seen as the "person to treat" in the family system and may be pushed into treatment or therapy. The reality is this child is reflecting the toxic issues in the family system by his or her behaviors. No one is looking beneath the child's behaviors to understand that they reflect the whole family and do not belong to just the child. In all likelihood, the whole family could be identified as the patient needing treatment or therapy to move from the toxic roles played out compulsively.

Later in life, Scapegoats may need to "divorce" themselves from their family of origin in order to form a better sense of self, along with a more realistic sense of who they are and how they contribute to the world. It will be important for these persons to pick their partners carefully and "avoid" choosing what is familiar and re-creating a family system that is similar to their family of origin.

Being the Scapegoat in this type of family system can also translate into problems in the workplace later in life. The Scapegoat child becomes the adult employee who sees issues in the workplace and points them out. If this is not seen as having value, and the workplace is toxic, the system of the toxic family is re-created in the workplace. If workplace colleagues occupy roles similar to those of the person's family system, the more familiar the situation feels—and the more toxic it can become. We often see family systems re-created in the workplace, each person trying to change what they were not able to do in their own family.

The Scapegoat Child

- The "problem child"
- Family toxicity or dysfunction is projected onto this child
- Carries blame and shame of the family
- Sees the reality of the dysfunction of the family and may point it out
- Feels the rejection of the family
- Often the first one to leave the family in some manner

The Scapegoat child offers the family:

- A place to point the blame and shame—inside the household
- A person to take anger out on
- A person to take rejection out on—a projection of how family members feel
- A person to point out to outsiders as the reason why the family has problems—not anyone else

Lost Child

Should there be more than two children, or if family roles change as the family system develops deeper or longer into toxic behaviors, one of its members may come to occupy the role of Lost child.

This is the child who learns it is better not to say anything or do anything that may cause conflict or negative attention in the family. Since little or no conflict or tension is coming from this child, he or she offers relief to others in the family. This child learns to take care of himself or herself and relies on material or tangible things to feel secure or valued. These children become agile at surviving situations and taking care of themselves without getting the attention of the family. When fighting or arguing occurs in the family, the Lost child avoids it by watching TV, playing video games, reading, or listening to music on headphones . . . doing anything other than engaging in the battle going on in the home.

Because of a lack of attention and nurturing, Lost children feel insecure at a deeper level than children in the other roles do. They feel they are so miniscule in the family that they do not even matter. No one in the family worries about them, so they are forgotten. They will often slide from the attention of others at school as well. As these persons grow older, they are often not thought of as someone who gives ideas or solutions on the job—since they are not really seen or heard there either. The Lost child often grows up to be an Avoider or Compromiser. With the Hero holding the stress of the family, and the Scapegoat holding the rejection of the family, the Lost child learns it is best not to enter the fray.

The Lost Child

- Learns not to say anything
- Learns to avoid family conflicts and lay low
- Learns to take care of himself or herself
- Relies on tangibles to feel secure (car, jewelry, "stuff")
- Avoids by watching TV, playing video games, reading, listening on earphones

The Lost child offers the family:

- A sense of no worries—family relief
- A person who carries the insecurities of the family (can't rely on anything that is not tangible)
- A backup when the other children are gone or away

Clown

The fourth role is a role not always determined by birth order or number of children in the family. It develops in some toxic family systems to offer stress relief to other family members. The Clown takes the pressure off in a highly pressurized family system. This role is the funny one in the family. This person learns that the best way around the stress and conflict in the family is to offer fun or silly comments, jokes, and behaviors.

This child learns to be funny at home, funny at school, and funny with friends. People in general like to be around this person, as the Clown offers everyone a sense of fun. The difficulty for these children as they become older is that they are not allowed to have their own stress, hurt, or fears. In fact, it is difficult for Clowns to identify their own feelings as they habitually "put on" a mask of having a great life full of fun, yet nothing could be further from the truth.

To be stuck in this role in the family, school, and later in the business world is to feel alone and inadequate. This is the child who worries about not being "good enough." The focus in life for this person is to find ways to take the stress off others. Often this person grows up to be an Accommodator, wanting to keep peace and make everyone happy.

The Clown Child

- The funny one in the family
- The clown at school and work
- Always trying to make others laugh
- Least aware of own feelings
- On the edge—will they be "funny enough"?
- Feels a sense of inadequacy

The Clown child offers the family:

- A sense of stress relief
- Takes the "pressure-cooker" effect off the family system
- Another means to take the focus off the family toxicity or dysfunction
- An excuse for outlandish behaviors

What These Roles Mean

None of these roles are "bad," and we all play them at times, given the situations we find ourselves in. The trouble comes when we are pressured to play one or two to meet the designated needs of our family system, and when we perform these roles compulsively to the point of being unhealthy.

These roles, along with the styles of conflict we tend to use, set us up for internal debates or self-talk inside our heads. At each point of conflict as adults, we dig up similar situations from our past and try to use these as a baseline for how to move forward. When these past situations were handled in a manner that was toxic or unhealthy, we try to resolve current situations by replaying the old dysfunctional dynamic over and over again, hoping for a different outcome. We are compelled to try to make it better, or different, and yet we do not have the correct tools to do so.

When we don't have new tools and techniques to change the outcome, then the same old outcomes happen time and again. More frustration develops, and depending on our style, we begin to blame others, ourselves, or both, and nothing really changes. This can lead to depression, isolation, and/or anger. If the tendency is depression (accommodate and avoid), then we could become so depressed that we turn inward and become suicidal. If the tendency is anger (compete), then we may become more and more explosive, causing harm to others—verbal, nonverbal, physical, emotional. Other people who live with Competers find methods to work around that person—like not responding, avoiding, and using passive-aggressive behaviors. Competers tend to be attracted to Accommodators or Avoiders since these persons give them more room to express themselves and offer less criticism regarding their behavior.

What Is a Blameless Relationship?

To create a blameless relationship with yourself is to understand the family system that you grew up in, and how that system affected you. Then, decide if you are still living with one of those roles attached to you in an unhealthy way. If you are, make a decision to take your inner power back and no longer live in that style compulsively. We all tend to repeat and live out those things that were unresolved in our childhoods—to try to make sense of them or to finish our feelings, so that we can move on.

No one leaves childhood without some issues; unfortunately, some people have more than others. Fortunately, we all have the ability to understand and change ourselves by peeling off the layers of toxic and dysfunctional behaviors and hurts. Underneath is the core of who we are and what we want to be. This is who we are working to let out into the light of day. And to do that, we must change our brains to become more consistent with that hidden part of us.

We do have the ability to change our brains! No longer do you need to blame yourself for your history of relationships lost or thrown off-kilter. Now you can practice how to become the hidden you until it's the only you—a little bit more each day. If you do not have a healthy relationship with *you*, it is very difficult to create a healthy relationship with someone else.

Undoing Toxic Family Roles

The survival skills we most likely learned in order to survive a toxic family are reactive (Competer, Accommodator, and Avoider). In a reactive style, we learn to blame ourselves or others or both. It's important to remember that you learned these toxic roles and behaviors because you had no other choice. They felt, and probably were, necessary to your survival. That makes them hard to let go of. This is especially seen in toxic vertical relationships in which one person is very dominant and the other person is submissive. Consider the reactions a dominant or submissive person feels when backed into a corner—how they fight to win, look to blame, find a way to avoid or smooth the conflict away. It feels and looks like a battle because when we're stuck in those roles, that's exactly what it is!

If we allow instinct and habit to guide us in our relationships, we most likely are going to end up blaming someone, ourselves, or both of us. That noise, or instinct, inside my head—*your* head— is the voice of Mom, Dad, grandparent, older brother, stepparent. Figuring out who you regularly share space with in your brain and how you can let go of those persons is the key to your own empowerment. It is not easy to change something as familiar as this pattern. Your investment in who you have become is large, even if you have lost relationships because of it. Seeking to do something different is risky and new. It takes self-analysis, insight, reflection, and the practice of doing something different, over and over again. However, with practice, the capacity for a blameless relationship with self and others is something worth struggling for.

To move from a reactive style to a proactive style means using "no-blame skills" such as

- solution-focused problem solving
- team building
- asking for and getting assistance with issues or problems

These skills can help you build healthy ongoing relationships with family, friends, colleagues, and especially with partners and significant others. They can be used to create equal-horizontal relationships that enable closeness and intimacy. They enable clear communication that is win-win focused. The ultimate goal of using these skills is to build a peaceful life by living and working in cooperation with others in all areas of your life.

Toxic or Not?

- None of these roles are "bad."
- We all play one or more of them at times.
- Often we play out these roles in our current situations in order to make sense of them in our own minds, or change them.
- These roles can be used in conflict—and we need to learn successful skills for successful relationships.
- These roles cause more grief in our minds as we try to sort out healthy behaviors.
- It's important not to play any role in a compulsive manner . . .
- . . . or expect others to be in the same one all the time.

To Create a Blameless Relationship with Yourself:

- Understand your family system.
- Understand how your family system affected you.
- Understand how you repeat those behaviors in your new system.
- Identify what you can change.
- Know you have the power to change.
- Create the change!

There are no corners to cut when your goals are mutual empowerment. To assist you in sorting out the roles you may have played in your family of origin, please see the exercises in this chapter. Review the roles described above and consider who in your family played which roles, including yourself. Ask yourself if people in your family were allowed to be fluid—to move in and out of roles—rather than having to compulsively play certain roles at different stages of the family history. Then, write down the roles you play in your current relationships (love, friendship, school, work) and analyze how those affect your life now. Are there mannerisms or behaviors that you feel would be helpful to change? Develop a plan of action to do so.

Family Role Exercise

Review the four roles (Hero, Scapegoat, Lost Child, and Clown) discussed in Big Idea 7, Create a Blameless Relationship with Yourself. Use the table below to record what roles were played by you and others in your family and to what degree or with what mannerisms.

Roles	Played by . . .	Degree/Mannerisms
Hero		
Scapegoat		
Lost Child		
Clown		

Ask yourself if any of these roles were lived out compulsively or if your family members moved in and out of these roles fluidly.

1. (Circle one) My family **was/was not** compulsive in the roles we played.

2. (Finish this sentence) My family was compulsive in the roles we played in the following ways:

_____

_____

Family Role Exercise continued

---

3. (Circle one) My family members **moved/did not move** fluidly from role to role.

Write down your analysis of the roles you play in your current relationships and how those roles affect your life.

4. (Circle one) In my developing years, I learned to deal with conflict in a **healthy/unhealthy** manner.

5. (Finish this sentence) I play the following roles in my current relationships, and those roles affect my life in the following ways:

_____

_____

List the mannerisms or behaviors that you feel need to be changed. Develop an action plan to change.

6. (Finish this sentence) It would be helpful for me to change the following mannerisms or behaviors:

_____

_____

7. (Finish this sentence) I will implement the following action plan to change the mannerisms or behaviors listed above:

_____

_____

BIG IDEA 8

Avoid Premature Forgiveness

In the last chapter, we talked about how the roles we played in our families of origin shaped our conflict styles. For example, family members who played the role of "Hero child" find it hard as adults to admit they're not perfect and don't have all the answers. In a conflict, they'll often take on the style of a Competer. In contrast, a "Scapegoat child" often grows up to be an Avoider, choosing to lie low so as not to repeat the pattern of being blamed. However, as discussed, the familiarity of these old roles is often the very thing that drives us to repeat the same painful cycles as an adult—that is, until and unless we choose to break free of the old impulsive thoughts and behaviors.

In this chapter, we look specifically at those who have the conflict style of accommodating, or not rocking the boat. When a disagreement makes the other person upset, the Accommodator's first response is to shut down. Accommodating makes it hard for a *we* solution to present itself and can be a major problem for both parties in the struggle.

Rather than face escalating conflict, this type of person issues premature forgiveness (a peacemaker at all costs). Accommodators are liable to adapt after a confrontation and pick up the pieces left by others. They are quick to smooth over any fallout, no matter how hurtful the experience. They act and often feel as though the only important thing is re-establishing harmony—or at least the semblance of harmony. They value the relationship above their own needs. They often leave the impression that they are tough and invulnerable, that they can take whatever is dished out. They hide any fear of their own needs not being met with an attitude of "no big deal." And yet . . . it is a big deal. Eventually, the Accommodator or Avoider will explode! One can only hold down hurt, frustration, or powerlessness so long before an explosion occurs—either on the inside or on the outside.

Not surprisingly, there appears to be a magnetic attraction between implosive people (Accommodators and Avoiders) and explosive people (Competers) in relationship, meaning someone who underreacts will likely end up in a relationship with someone who overreacts. If Competers push an issue or argument and explode in anger, they will usually provoke an emotional shutdown in their partners. In response, they may back off for a moment—perhaps even make some sort of apology in the wake of that explosive moment. And that's when the Avoider or Accommodator will spring forth with an expression of premature forgiveness. If the Competer apologizes, the Accommodator or Avoider will say, "I'm sorry, too. It's okay now—let's forget about it."

If this is your tendency, learning how and why to avoid premature forgiveness will help you learn to bite your lip and do something different! If you are the Competer in your relationship, please read, reflect, and decide if it is time to change.

The Cost of Premature Forgiveness

By forgiving prematurely, the Accommodator or Avoider passes up an opportunity to ask for what is needed, which is mutual accountability and joint problem solving. So let's look again at what just happened. The Competer behaved self-indulgently by saying hurtful things or behaving in inconsiderate ways. The Accommodator or Avoider probably grew quiet and put up some emotional walls. But now the ugliness of the scene has come and gone. As the intensity of the conflict subsides, the Competer may have second thoughts about the outburst. As the Avoider or Accommodator, you want to indulge the Competer by offering quick and complete forgiveness, but beware. Set a goal for yourself in the future: Keep the conversation going. Do not fold and automatically take on the role of peacemaker, selling yourself and the relationship short.

Avoiding Premature Forgiveness

- The first response of a peacemaker in a conflict or disagreement is to shut down . . .
- or work quickly to smooth it over.
- This is a major problem in close or intimate relationships.
- Avoiders or Accommodators act as if the most important thing is to re-establish harmony . . .
- which ends up happening at their and the other person's expense.

Once the heat of conflict is behind you, your job is to keep the conversation going. How do you do this? You might start by saying that you don't like what happened and you want to see something different in the future. You can make a request for a different and healthier exchange. Here are some examples:

"Okay, we can talk about forgiveness. However, I do not want to go through this kind of ugly scene again."

"What can you do the next time to interrupt yourself before you say [or do] all those mean things to me?"

Resist blaming or shaming. Make it clear that you both share responsibility for solving the problem and causing a change in behavior.

Pitfalls and Hidden Meanings

It is important for Accommodators or Avoiders to understand that their needs are important. Learning to maintain personal regard for self is essential if they're going to have a chance at changing their behaviors to be more *we-centered* versus *other-centered*. You may be unaware of the underlying meaning in statements such as "I'm sorry" and "You're forgiven." Allow the subsurface truths about these comments to slow down your impulse to take care of others the next time you're tempted to quickly accommodate the other person's discomfort and smooth things over.

When Accommodators or Avoiders say, "I'm sorry!" they often mean one of the following:

- "I want you to excuse me from the responsibility of having to figure out what to do to help solve this problem. You do it and leave me out of it."

- "Your needs are more important than my needs. I do not deserve to have my needs met."

- "No matter what the price, I just want this hassle to be over!"

- "You're right! (You're a better debater than I am.) Watch for the next time around, though—I will still be fuming over this unresolved issue!"

- "You win this time—but I will get you, sometime and somehow!"

- "You owe me now that I'm acting so humble."

- "If you truly loved me, you would offer me some forgiveness too."

- "My responsibility is to make you feel loved. (Never mind that I don't feel loved.)."

In any of these responses, the Accommodators or Avoiders not only subjugate themselves to the other person, but they also back out of taking responsibility for the situation by not participating in a solution. Further down the road, this can lead to "blame-you" behaviors that end in statements like one or more of these:

- "You never listen to me and all I was trying to do was help."
- "Now look at the mess you created!" (At this point getting in their own jab of self-righteousness from their passive-aggressive behavior.)

Martyrdom comes in many faces, and letting go, seemingly, of the need to feel important or cared for is another negative outcome of relationship conflict. Giving up the right to feel valued in relationship gives the limbic brain the chance to push its self-pity button. When the limbic feels bad, it wants to feel better. It will go to its memory bank to think about what makes it feel better: alcohol, drugs, sex, gambling, food, new clothes, sporting gear . . . the list goes on. Off we go to "get me some of that thing!" A relapse is born in this "not-feeling-cared-for" period. This cycle repeats over and over again, with the limbic consistently looking to be soothed.

When you close an argument by simply saying, "You're forgiven," what you often really mean is

- "I can live with your behavior the way it is."
- "Getting to a solution can wait."
- "As long as you ultimately see the error of your ways, and I know you're trying, then that's enough for me (until the next time)."
- "I do not like the feeling of the relationship being under stress, so let's hurry through this ugly part and get on with the better or happy part!"
- "I'm scared to ask for equality in the relationship. I'm not even sure if I deserve it (self-blame)."

The notions of mutual understanding, mutual respect, and mutual winning do not find a home in the limbic system. So, you may wonder, where is the cortex in this encounter between chronic Competers and chronic Avoiders or Accommodators? The Accommodators/Avoiders want so much to under-react to any potentially tense or stressful situation, they are willing to reject themselves. This behavioral script gets dug so deeply in their limbic brains that, when a conflict is even hinted at, they instinctually avoid any of the unsettling emotions that come with expressing their own needs or feelings. Of course, what is lost is the possibility of taking this problem or disagreement to a *mutual* resolution.

If you are an implosive person facing an explosive partner, you have no tolerance for disagreements. When the other person is asking to be forgiven, you feel compelled to absorb his or her discomfort as well as your own, and assume that the relationship is increasingly in jeopardy the longer the discomfort lasts. That is when *you* need to resist and apply Big Idea 8 to the situation by *avoiding premature forgiveness*! You are in such a hurry to bring ugly scenes to a conclusion, you allow the other person off the hook, and nothing gets solved. Your challenge is to stand still in the moment, and resist this temptation.

There is one goal we need to set for ourselves, and that is to keep the conversation going. Even though you can see the other person is uncomfortable and regrets what he or she did or said, you must keep the spotlight on the situation a bit longer. A teachable moment is at hand. You are the only one who can ask the other party to participate in creating a mutual solution. Keep in mind, this is not about right and wrong or even about forgiveness. This is about mutual problem solving. Working together is the way out of this maze of premature forgiveness!

Changing Premature Forgiveness

- As the under-reactor, you need to bite your lip to keep from saying the usual "I forgive yous."

- Keep the conversation going, or take a break and agree to come back to the conversation when things have cooled and the cortex is engaged.

- Say what you don't like—words, behaviors—and what you want to see different in the future.

- Make a request for a behavior change in the other person.

- Share the responsibility of solving the problem by changing your behavior too.

- Your needs are important. Stick to the *we* and not the *you.*

Premature Forgiveness Exercise

1. Describe the person who is the premature forgiver in your life.

   _____

   _____

   _____

2. Describe the truths and fears behind the apologies and expressions of forgiveness most often used. (For example, *"They will leave me if I don't give in, and I can't have that."*)

   _____

   _____

   _____

   _____

   _____

3. Describe how you can help to keep the conversation going (if you are the premature forgiver) or how you can move toward mutual solution creation (if you are the Competer). How can you change these behaviors in order to get to a normal relationship?

   _____

   _____

   _____

   _____

   _____

BIG IDEA 9

Put Down Your Dukes

In the previous chapter, we discussed the importance of avoiding premature forgiveness. This raised certain implied subtruths—what might be going on below the surface when you forgive someone too soon. I listed some strategies to keep the conversation going instead of falsely saying "I forgive you." The concepts of self-regard and soothing the limbic system by building a pathway to the cortex were covered. The actions of requesting a change in behavior and staying in those moments to allow the other person to share in mutual problem solving—or solution-focused thinking—was another key point. Again, we were reminded that it takes time and effort to build these new pathways in the brain—and the more thoughtful behaviors they produce.

In this chapter, we look at competitive instinct and the process involved in "taking down your dukes." When people get angry, take the offensive, and attack somebody verbally, it can be abusive and intimately hurtful. There's no way of ignoring this type of explosion. It's literally and figuratively "right in your face."

It makes sense that Competers are the ones who respond to conflict in this over-reactive way. However, as you learned earlier,

Avoiders and Accommodators can ultimately resort to this kind of behavior as well. No matter what conflict style they usually exhibit, when people implode or explode and point the finger, they have invested in the belief that "the best defense is a strong offense."

All styles of conflict have their own unique style of defending. Big Idea 9, Put Down Your Dukes, encourages us to look at the cumulative effect of *defense* (not just defense masquerading as offense) as the major source of the damage we do to the people who matter most to us.

When all is said and done, the behaviors that kill the most promising of relationships are putting up your dukes, getting defensive, cutting off attempts at communication, and arguing with a partner about whose needs take priority. This is the case regardless of whether the words or actions are delivered in an over- or under-reactive way. When you respond to significant others by trying to blame and control in emotional moments, it's the beginning of the end. From that moment on, the honeymoon is over and might never be heard from or felt again. When you start treating someone (whether it's you or somebody else) as "the bad guy," or as someone deserving of punishment, you've invited a continental divide into the relationship. The goal is to stop, take your own inventory, and then start taking steps to change this impulsive, reactive pattern.

Yes, But Why Are We Like This?

The fighting style that most of us use (being quick to dismiss, minimize, turn things around, cross-examine, be critical or punitive, or throw cold shoulders) is the opposite of mutual problem-solving/solution-focused behavior. You may wonder why your relationships, even the ones that start so well, go south so frequently. Reactiveness does not appear as a problem behavior until the honeymoon is over—when both parties stop trying to impress each other.

Up to this point, both of you have tried to create the impression that you are worthy of the relationship and worth staying with, and that, in fact, you do not need much to make you happy. You're a "low-maintenance" kind of gal or guy! When disillusion sets in, because the couple has grown past the Honeymoon period, real-life issues come into play. In the stages of relationships, you'll recall we named this the Disillusionment stage. It's exactly when what we truly need and want in order to be in relationship needs to be discussed.

Have I Been Tricked?

It needs to be said and understood that no one person is to blame for this "deception," that is, the movement from Honeymoon to Disillusionment. It happens in every relationship, and every participant in a relationship is accountable for moving out of honeymoon and into disillusion. Each of you now must decide and declare what you need to be in relationship with the other. Consider that this is the usual process relationships go through. How we deal with it (or don't deal with it) is up to each one of us. And the place to begin is within you. What do you need from this person? Equally important is listening to the other. The activity of being with our partner, significant other, children, family members, friends, or colleagues and discovering what they need from us to be in relationship is just as important, if not more so, than sharing our needs with him or her. It is a two-way communication, and you can lead the way with the other person. It is about the *we*.

Perhaps it is obvious by now, but this is not an easy process. Not when we've lived so much of our lives not knowing and/ or not sharing what we really need emotionally. The fact is that everyone figures out what they want through a process of elimination. We become aware of what we don't want long before we achieve any significant level of insight into what we do want. Hate or discomfort gets our attention long before we have a clue about what we affirm and whom we hold dear.

When Needs Don't Match

When our partners' needs and wants include something that we've eliminated from our own list of wants, we tend to correct them emphatically. To drive the point home, we might resort to angry outbursts, cold shoulders, or unflattering comparisons. We point out that we are more attentive to their needs than they are to ours.

Our partners, who are no more evolved in the identification of what they need and want than we are, defend themselves or go on the attack. Battle lines are drawn, and couples start resorting increasingly to fight-or-flight survival strategies. A "War of the Roses" ensues and the honeymoon swiftly moves from disillusion to misery, until death do they part.

These different needs weren't always a problem in our relationships. In the beginning, opposites attracted. Later on, when we started trying to change our partners, the real friction began. Things that attracted us to the other person no longer do. They become points of contention. That's when we start trying to force our partners to see how contrary their needs are to what we desire. For example, we might say: "I'm not going to sit around this house night after night, huddled together in front of the TV. We never get out and have fun anymore. You're so predictable and boring. I can't stand it!"

Partners hearing these complaints might defend the flip side of the equation just as vehemently. "You'd rather spend time with total strangers than spend time with me! You said you wanted to develop a quality relationship, then you never want to stay home and work on developing it. You're shallow! You never want to talk and share hopes and dreams like you did when we first started dating. I don't think you love me as much as I love you!"

And on and on. Gridlock sets in when we roll out the words *always* and *never,* red flags that we've entered the blame-and-shame game.

How We "Put Up Our Dukes"

- We start out in the Honeymoon stage of relationships and kiss up to each other.

- We move into Disillusionment—real life comes into play, and the styles of communication and family-of-origin issues come to the front of the relationship.

- Opposites attract, and what was an attractor is now a detractor.

- Misery sets in—along with blame for the deception. "You are not the prince (or princess) I started out with!"

- Our dukes are up—we're ready to fight in the way that's most comfortable for us!

- This is when the Four Fabulous Agreements come in—if we could only figure out what we really want.

Telltale Signs of Disillusion

Defend, explain away, minimize, or refuse to acknowledge. These are the activities couples engage in after the honeymoon is over. After the easy part of getting to know one another is over, couples rarely have conversations in which they explore how to achieve mutual need fulfillment. They act as though it's an "either/or" proposition. Instead of figuring out how both of them can have some, or slightly more, of what they want, they engage in pitched battles, some hot and some cold, in an effort to force the other person to "get over it" and give up some of his or her personal needs. Both partners spend time and energy working so hard to eliminate the negative from their relationship that they forget to accentuate the positive. They act as though it's all or nothing. "I win and get what I want, or you win and I don't." Black-and-white thinking. Not a match made in heaven!

The following are examples of how different conflict styles put up their dukes:

Competers

Competers crawl behind a wall of fire and resentment. "You should have known how upset that would make me," they say. "You're just being selfish!" They turn around your requests for fulfillment, blaming you for having too many items on your wish list and causing you to feel needy and greedy. They are the first ones to state publicly what they don't want and to find fault with what is on your list of wants. More often than not, they lack the insight to articulate exactly what would meet the needs they just stated. They engage in control struggles and try to emotionally arm-wrestle us out of our needs. This process rarely creates satisfaction for anybody, and both partners tend to become angrier and less fulfilled over time. A major reason for this is that the Competer pushes people away and treats them so unkindly that these poor souls no longer want to give anything in return.

Avoiders

Avoiders hide behind a wall of ice. "I work my fingers to the bone trying to pay for a happy home life. If you're going to complain all the time when I'm here, I'm going back to the office or out with friends, where I'm appreciated." Avoiders withhold their affection if they aren't satisfied. They dish out cold shoulders when they think others' needs are taking over and crowding out their own. Because they shy away from confrontation, they rarely put what they want on the table. They're liable to expect us to read their minds in order to figure out what we should do to make them happy. "There shouldn't be any problem with me having what I want," they think. They act as though the relationship is defective if there is even the slightest hint that needs and wants must be talked about and negotiated. They refuse to engage in the basic maintenance work necessary to keep relationships fresh and alive. Ultimately, they do not want to be hurt! They suffer from the "Avoider's Dream"—the unrealistic belief that somewhere out there is this perfect relationship in which there will be absolutely no conflict.

Accommodators

Accommodators hide behind a wall of guilt. "I try so hard to please you, and what does it get me? Nothing!" they're heard saying on a regular basis. "I try to keep dinner warm even when you don't come home on time. You could at least call and give me the respect of letting me know when your plans change." They like to compare our shoddy efforts to their own excessive attempts to please. They fuss about how difficult we make the job of pleasing them. As far as putting their own needs on the table, they act like they don't have any. They act invulnerable and as though their sole purpose in life is to serve. This means they don't do a good job of holding up their end during mutual problem-solving/solution-focused discussions. Needs fulfillment, especially their own, is extremely difficult for them because they are the last ones to say aloud what will make them happy. They're so totally caught up in pleasing everyone else that they honestly might not know their own needs.

So, come on—put down your dukes! Lead with your transparencies. Take the Big Ideas and apply these in place of your usual style. You can win battle after battle with the fire, ice, or guilt you throw, only to be left in the ring alone after fewer than ten rounds. Do not expect people to remain in the ring for the years and years that your grandparents or even parents have. This is a much less tolerant society. People move on when they do not feel successful or have some sense of accomplishment or fulfillment. We are a *now* society as well. The limbic has low impulse control. People want to see things happen quickly. Sometimes, the speed to which we think that we or others are able to change (or *should* be able to change) is unrealistic.

Intimacy: "In-to-me-see"

The truly courageous person makes an effort to be as transparent as possible when communicating with those who matter most. Angry, competitive people are not being courageous; they are hiding behind a wall of fire, acting cocksure and invulnerable. Folks who avoid are acting just as invulnerable, hunkered down behind their wall of ice. What goes around comes around. By stringing barbed wire and tucking our vulnerability away for safekeeping, we encourage our significant others to do the same. No meaningful communication takes place when this happens. Everyone starts defending themselves and spelling out all the ways in which their positions are non-negotiable. The term *intimacy* can be broken down into four interconnecting words: "in-to-me-see."

Remember, whether we are over-reacting or under-reacting, we are taking steps to cover up what we truly think and feel, stopping others from getting a glimpse at our vulnerability. The fragile flower of intimacy will not survive in relationships where people are not brave enough to "put down their dukes" and stop blaming and controlling.

How to Develop "In-To-Me-See"

- Lead with your transparencies.
- Take the Ten Big Ideas and use them daily.
- Remain—hang in there—and build your spiritual, emotional, physical, and psychological self.
- Influence the potential change in the relationship by establishing the change in you.
- Remember that no relationship is perfect—we all must work to get to better relationships.
- It is a lifelong journey.

It is important here to remember the phrase "Hang in there!" Do not drop out of the relationship too quickly. If the relationship has loyalty, a chance for change, and a sense of integrity (no physical, sexual, financial, emotional abuse), do not pack your bags and look for another spot to land. Your bags will always be with you, and it is highly likely you would be bringing with you the unresolved issues from your past relationship(s). No relationship is perfect, and you must decide if this one is worth working out. Influence the change in the relationship by your own change. By your change, you give others in your life the chance to change, and the example of how to do so. Lead by example. When you change, it is likely to affect the other person in the relationship to change. The rules are no longer the same. Change almost has to happen.

Stress and Violence: How It Affects the Brain

Stress is caused by internal pressures that build up each day in the natural course of exposing ourselves to our environment. Stress is natural and takes on many forms, but these forms all have a common pattern, from biological stressors to emotional stressors. Stress is also caused by a buildup of past experiences projected onto current situations, especially if those past experiences are the source of a deep hurt or an unresolved issue. These stressors are particular to each person's background and personal history.

As discussed in Big Idea 6, all stresses have a cycle. The cycle of stress is moving from a peaceful state to an uncomfortable state and back to a peaceful state. An uncomfortable state is not a negative state—it's just a state that is other than peaceful.

Figure 4. Stress Cycle

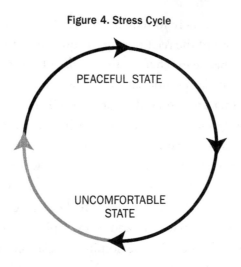

PEACEFUL STATE

UNCOMFORTABLE
STATE

Bio-stressors

Bio-stressors are biological forces that act on the body. Some examples of bio-stressors are listed below.

- gas buildup in the stomach and/or intestines
- urine buildup in the bladder
- feces buildup in the bowel
- dust buildup in the nose
- phlegm in the throat
- hot or cold temperatures
- physical pain
- itches and irritations
- viruses, colds, diseases
- nausea in the stomach
- inactivity

Emotional Stressors

Emotional stressors are emotional forces that act on the body. Some examples of emotional stressors are listed below.

- joy
- grief
- terror
- shame
- embarrassment
- frustration
- anger
- inadequacy
- jealousy (specifically the fear of being abandoned)
- envy (specifically the fear of being inadequate or "not good enough")
- extreme boredom
- helplessness
- resentment (anger and/or hurt hidden or repressed)
- humor
- loneliness
- sexual needs
- hurt
- fear (nervousness, anxiety, hyper-vigilance)
- denial and repression (keeping something secret)

Emotional stressors move a person from a peaceful state to an uncomfortable state and, depending on the course of action chosen, back to a peaceful state again.

The uncomfortable state is referred to as the "stress response." A stress response is made up of the internal pressures and/or anxieties that the body feels a need to expel during the course of each day. The stress response is nature's cue for a person to move into a course of action. The goal is to move the body from an uncomfortable state back to a peaceful state.

However, it is our perception of a situation, because of our emotional fabric, that causes us to see it as "Our Reality," when in fact it may not be what's really going on. In some situations, a person might find that an old insecurity is triggered by a stress response. This triggering sets off old, and often destructive, attitudes and behaviors that result in contaminating the situation at hand.

To illustrate this, the following example is taken from the real-life situation of a couple in a romantic relationship. We will call them Nora and Jake.

Nora and Jake

At some point in Nora and Jake's relationship, Jake had affairs with other women when he was drinking or drugging. Nora had affairs as well when she was drinking or drugging. Both see their own life situation as a by-product of their using, yet still have lingering feelings of hurt and shame. Nora's parents divorced because of her father's affairs, and Nora feels deep, unresolved pain from the loss of her parents' marriage. She also has past and current insecurity issues surrounding men hurting her and then leaving her and feels a loss of control over what happens in her life.

Thoughts Seen As Real

Nora is driving to an appointment on her lunch hour and sees Jake in the parking lot near a hotel, with a beautiful redheaded woman. Her first thought is, "Oh no, who is that?" She then begins to think in her limbic brain, "She is much more beautiful than I am." Nora starts to worry, as she and Jake have not been getting along so well lately. She starts to suspect this woman is in a relationship with Jake and they are just going into or coming out of the hotel. Her thoughts become real to her.

Insecurity

She begins to lose awareness that this is just a thought, not based on truth or inquiry. She begins to see this perception as real and believes it beyond a shadow of a doubt. She then expects that because this woman is more beautiful, and most likely more fun than she is, Jake would easily go to the hotel with her. Nora is now taking these thoughts seriously, and she continues to validate her insecurities and stress by obsessing on the arguments she and Jake have been experiencing lately.

Focusing on Details

Nora comes home that night and is furious, yet not able to share her feelings of insecurity. She watches Jake carefully to see how he responds to her when he comes home. She does not notice the emotional blockade she has built, but when he enters the door her face is full of anger and hostility. Jake runs upstairs to take a shower. This only focuses Nora's suspicions.

Triggers Habit and Situation Worsens

This preoccupation triggers Nora's old habits of nagging and complaining in order to cope with insecure feelings. Nora tells Jake he needs to be more attentive and loving. Jake is tired, he is not communicating, and he is avoiding the conversation. Jake's response (or lack of response) only worsens Nora's negative and insecure feelings and reactions.

Thoughts Validated

As the night wears on, Nora tries to engage Jake in lovemaking. He says he's too tired. This further validates her thoughts and suspicions. Nora has a terrible night and feels hurt, abandoned, and alone. She only wants things to be the same as before that awful redheaded woman entered the picture.

Burnout!

In the morning, Nora gets up and makes coffee for the two of them, as usual. Jake comes downstairs and says, "I have no time for coffee—gotta run to an early morning appointment. See ya." Jake starts to leave, and Nora yells to Jake, "Don't bother coming back tonight!" Jake is confused. He is wondering where this is coming from. By this time, Nora is in the "burnout" stage of stress. She has come to believe that Jake is having an affair. The relationship is over, so she might as well end it now. Up to this point, Nora has not spoken one word about seeing Jake in the hotel parking lot or that she saw him with another woman.

To break this cycle of stress is simple, but it's not easy. First, Nora would do better to consider standing still in the moment with her feelings of insecurity. She might validate her feelings by becoming aware of how they're based in the past. At this point it is best for Nora to make a call to Jake and let go of her fear and insecurity. She might tell Jake that she saw him in a hotel parking lot with a beautiful redhead, and that this caused her immediate feelings of insecurity. Nora might also admit that seeing Jake with the woman is triggering old thoughts and feelings about her parents' divorce, as well as her past relationships, and that she's worried it's happening again. It's best to describe how she is feeling rather than blaming or shaming Jake, which will only lead to his defending himself, and the conversation will be at a standstill; or worse, it will move to a place of competitiveness.

If Nora were to approach it this way, transparently, he might say, "Yes, honey, I was in that parking lot with a beautiful redhead, and next to that parking lot is a Mexican restaurant where we went to have lunch. The redhead is my cousin, who had called me earlier that morning to say she was in town and to invite me to lunch. I knew you had a lunch appointment, so I didn't bother to call you."

Wow, what a difference this makes in contrast to Nora's old triggered behaviors and insecurities. She can decide to believe Jake and, since there is no recent history or reason to disbelieve him, she and Jake can move forward with their relationship in a healthy manner. The cycle of stress ends at that very moment, and they can both move on knowing they were able to discuss this situation and believe in one another.

This story is not an unusual one for people who have lived in addiction and trauma. Many of us live this type of experience periodically. The important thing is how we handle it, and when we end the cycle of stress. Only by addressing the stress and advising the other person can you resolve the stress before it becomes

Figure 5. Cycle of Stress and Violence

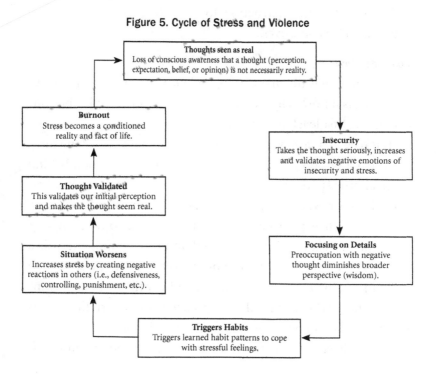

Thoughts seen as real
Loss of conscious awareness that a thought (perception, expectation, belief, or opinion) is not necessarily reality.

Burnout
Stress becomes a conditioned reality and fact of life.

Insecurity
Takes the thought seriously, increases and validates negative emotions of insecurity and stress.

Thought Validated
This validates our initial perception and makes the thought seem real.

Situation Worsens
Increases stress by creating negative reactions in others (i.e., defensiveness, controlling, punishment, etc.).

Focusing on Details
Preoccupation with negative thought diminishes broader perspective (wisdom).

Triggers Habits
Triggers learned habit patterns to cope with stressful feelings.

ɔbsessive. If you are worried you'll be fooled, it may be better to put your energy into believing—knowing that the truth will eventually come out, and that you have supportive friends in your recovery group to lean on.

Levels of Violence

When we are in the middle of feeling stress and we lose conscious awareness that our perceptions may not be reality, there is a real chance that we might move toward violence. Violence often starts very small, from a minor attitude or small behavior to a more serious level. It is vital to know the levels of violence and to be self-aware of our own attitudes and behaviors that, if built up, will cause destruction to others as well as ourselves.

> **There are four levels of violence:**
> - inconsideration
> - rejection
> - sabotage
> - destruction

Inconsideration

Inconsideration is the first level of violence. It seems like an everyday thing, is it not? Why would this attitude and behavior be considered the first level of violence?

It is true that "accidental inconsideration" happens all the time, like when a person goes through a door and doesn't look behind to see another person coming. This is an accidental inconsideration. However, when people are purposefully inconsiderate, they are aware of their poor behavior yet they choose to do it anyway. This type of behavior is self-centered and ego-bound, and it is a means of exerting control and power over another person. If an individual is inconsiderate to others, and continues being inconsiderate, that individual is exhibiting a behavior pattern that devalues others. Devaluing others is a form of violence.

This behavior is hurtful and harmful to others because it is thoughtless. If a person can be inconsiderate to others, it is easier for him or her to move to the second level of violence—rejection.

Rejection

Rejection is another form of self-centeredness. When individuals use rejection, their ego allows them to justify treating others in a harmful manner. The act of rejection is a level of violence that further devalues another person; in other words, one person displaces the worth of the person being rejected. When an individual is able to reject another and cause that person to feel a sense of worthlessness, it furthers the individual's inner belief that he or she has power and control over other people. The person doing the rejecting may feel somehow "better, smarter, or more skilled" than the other person.

Those on the receiving end of rejection might internalize this feeling and think they have less meaning or value in the world. This reaction is especially true if they are in a close relationship with the person. Rejection can bring on feelings of unworthiness, depression, desperation, and self-destruction. The consequences of rejection are of a higher emotional and spiritual level. Think back to the styles of conflict, and one might see Competers using this behavior as part of their lifestyle because they have more regard for self than for others. They believe this is how they are supposed to act in order to achieve the status and power they want. Nice guys or gals finish last, and Competers want none of that! They are often attracted to the Accommodator or Avoider and may run these first two levels of violence on a continuous basis.

Sabotage

If an individual can be inconsiderate and rejecting of others, could that person not sabotage other people? Yes, the next level of violence is sabotage.

Sabotage can take a variety of forms. It includes hurting someone's chance or opportunity to win or receive a promotion. It can be the act of saying something hurtful and potentially harmful to another person, like gossip. It can be the act of taking something away from the person, such as stealing.

Sabotage is an active behavior. It is a plotting activity that requires time and effort. During the planning phase, the saboteur could decide to abort the behavior.

Harm is intended at this level of violence. The continuation of the sabotaging behavior is a direct attempt at power and control. It is meant to take something away from another. It is targeted toward another person with the intention to be of harm. The level of consequence for this type of behavior is even higher than the last level of violence, as it is more active, is more deliberate, and requires a longer period of thought and planning.

Destruction

The last level of violence is destruction, which often is the first level that people consider to be violence. Destruction is the intent to tear a person down completely, to the point of destroying his or her spirit, dreams, hope, property, and/or life. This is power and control to the final degree—the perpetrator can willingly destroy or kill another person. To destroy means that the perpetrator believes that he or she has the right to completely obliterate another person. This type of behavior is pathological. A mental illness (for example, sociopathic or psychopathic mental illness, severe narcissism) or a toxic level of chemicals allows the perpetrator to justify his or her behavior.

Think about the times and situations when you have been inconsiderate, rejecting, sabotaging, or destructive. Often these are behaviors we learned in our families or from our peers. They can be a survival mechanism. However, once we are aware of these patterns in ourselves and in others, we are accountable and responsible to do something to change them in a more positive direction. If we demonstrate these attitudes and behaviors, it is helpful to seek counseling or support to change them. If our loved ones demonstrate these attitudes and behaviors, we need to address them (if it is not too dangerous to do so) or move away from the situation or person. These attitudes and behaviors are toxic.

People learn these types of behaviors and continue to use them as the benefits seem to outweigh the risks. There are "payoffs" or results that are welcomed because of this type of behavior. It may be status in a group as the "tough guy or gal," it may be receiving special consideration from others because of fear or misguided respect. When violent people receive these payoffs, it is more difficult to change the behavior. Violent people see the need to change only when their personal power or image is diminished. Some type of drastic experience has to happen to violent persons to break this cycle and cause them to reconsider their behavior. People can change—up to a certain point—and there are some who will not or feel they cannot. These really are few, however, in my experience.

Consider if any of these attitudes and behaviors are within you, whether you want to continue in these violent paths, or whether you want to redirect your behavior to engage in a healthier and more harmonious lifestyle.

Growing Up Violent

My first year of life was marked by the inconsiderate behavior of my mother, who left three children in a house unattended during her runaway escape. Through the years, family inconsideration and rejection brought more violence into my life. As I experienced this, I began to mirror it to others. I became rejecting of others and violent to boys particularly. Part of this was because of the physical and sexual abuse others were inflicting on me. I learned to fight and inflict pain on others to reduce my own. I deliberately sabotaged those I thought were out to get me. It seemed normal to take the behaviors that were inflicted on me and translate them to others, a vicious circle of my destruction. In recovery, I have learned to be aware of these tendencies and to change my attitude and behaviors at the first signs of inconsideration or rejection. No longer relying on these defense mechanisms to live my life has meant freeing up the need to hold on to the hurts and power they once had in my brain. Developing a new mind—a mind of caring for others, inner peace, and seeing the beauty in others—has replaced the old mind. Changing and developing is very thoughtful work and starts with the seemingly small inconsiderations in life.

The Three Reins in My Life

One realization I have made in my life is this: Who or what reigns in my life? In my worldview, I have a Higher Power, and with that spiritual piece in my life, I am able to turn the reins over to Him. I can't do this 100 percent of the time; however, compared to how uncontrolled and chaotic my life was before, it is so much better! When I turned my life over to a Power greater than myself, I could allow the wisdom of my Higher Power to reign. When I took back the reins, it felt like downpours of cold, hurtful rain!

I have learned that I prefer the soft, warm rain that comes when I use my cortex and turn my life over to my Higher Power. I have learned to rain love on others. When I rain love, love grows, and life is full!

Reining in my brain has been work—that is for sure! Most of the time, with the help of these skills and my Higher Power, it is possible. Now, there are times I choose not to. And I am careful about when, why, and for how long I let my limbic take over. Even then, quick recovery is vital so that my limbic reactions do not become familiar again.

Remember, self-control is not a natural instinct. It is learned. Some people learn higher levels of self-control by the discipline they are taught or witness as children. Still others grow up in families where they witness little or no self-discipline and their behaviors consequently demonstrate low impulse control. Learning a higher level of impulse control truly is a "brain choice."

As you work to make your own life healthier, and that of your family, you will create a new culture in your household. The next generation will benefit when you create new patterns of health in your life, and in the lives of those around you. Just as generational dysfunction cycles in families, so does generational recovery and functioning. It starts with you! Why you? Because you are reading this *now*, learning this information. You are becoming accountable for what you learn and apply to your life to improve the lives of future generations in your family.

Ground Rules for Conflict Resolution

Rules for fair fighting follow. Look them over with your partner or spouse and agree to abide by these rules in conflict and thus avoid putting up your dukes.

1. I am critical of ideas, not individuals. I do not judge you. I realize I am reacting to an energy, thought, or action. For example, I disagree with what you are saying, or I do not like what you did—not you as a person.

2. I take responsibility for how I communicate my differences with you. I am responsible for cooling myself down, choosing how I communicate, working through my projections, and so forth.

3. I focus on coming to the best decision, not on winning. I remember that we are all in this together.

4. I watch how my voice sounds when I communicate with you. Shouting or raising my voice only alienates us.

5. I give you time to express your side, your perceptions, and your reasons for doing or saying what you did. I realize you might not want to communicate if in the past we have not been able to "fight fairly." I also realize that you might not be at the place where you want or know how to communicate your viewpoints or perceptions with me, and that is okay. I am responsible for how I communicate my feelings and how I treat you, not how you communicate and act. However, I can choose to separate myself from you if you continue to be abusive, since I have chosen to stop being an abusive person to myself and to you.

6. I actively try to understand your viewpoint without giving in to yours or changing my own. By doing this, I allow you to be you and me to be me. Perhaps by doing this, we can experience a new level of intimacy, relationship, or trust.

7. I change my mind when evidence indicates that I should do so.

8. I understand that all conflict is an opportunity to learn about myself; therefore, I treat conflict as a positive experience in my life to help me grow stronger in my ability to express my feelings, learn appropriate boundaries, value myself, value others and their point of view, and communicate effectively and honestly with others.

9. Ultimately, I see you with love and respect, knowing that I want to keep in my heart and mind positive regard for you as a person in my life. To that end, I will use all Ten Big Ideas to assist me in working through our conflicts.

BIG IDEA 10

Take Responsibility for Self-Fulfilling Prophecies

Self-fulfilling prophecies—what are they and how do they work? In moments of conflict with our significant others, we bring a lot of tendencies with us that we initially deny are there, and, more often than not, we refuse to examine them. And this is true for most people who are new to cooperative problem solving in relationships. When we're experiencing confusion or emotional pain, we really dislike looking at ourselves as the "problem." Someone or something else gets the blame for whatever is wrong.

Before we tackled the ideas in this book, when we faced a relationship conflict, it was typical to play the role of victim, one who is either depressed or angry, depending on our conflict style. We were blind to the power we possessed to create our own worst fears. We didn't realize that we have the capacity to turn a difficult situation better or worse depending on our expectations of what is "supposed" to happen next. One of my favorite "laugh lines" in this sort of work is "Pack your bags; we're going on a guilt trip!"

Who Me, Worst Fears?

We all start out with "worst fears." Somewhere in the back (or front) of our minds is the fear of abandonment, being smothered, being taken advantage of, or growing bored in a close relationship. If any of these things actually begin to happen, we initially believe it's without any active participation of our own. It always seems to happen, somehow, *to* us. The nature of self-fulfilling prophecies is that, over time, as they happen to us again and again, we become convinced of our own mind-reading abilities and predictive powers.

Acknowledging our own responsibility in the creation of our own worst nightmares tends to come later in adulthood, if ever. Our role in shaping events with what we bring to the table is initially blocked from our view. Self-insight takes time to develop. It isn't there as we're growing up. In Twelve Step recovery, the most challenging step in the process is often taking a fearless inventory of ourselves because it involves developing a deeper understanding of how we shape our own destiny.

Here's an example of what we might tell ourselves: "I knew you were going to leave me! I knew it the first time you stayed here overnight and couldn't wait to leave the next morning. I knew the day would come when I'd never see you again. I figured you kept coming back just because it was convenient. You'd do a drive-by and dish out a little attention, then be on your merry way again. Get out of here! I know your type. I had you figured out the minute I first laid eyes on you!"

We can say all these things and still be unaware of how we are actively pushing the other person away—how we are creating the very outcome we dread. And it happens to us over and over again, never figuring out how we've added to the push.

This is the definition of a self-fulfilling prophecy!

Maturity Paves the Way for Healing Old Wounds

For the most part, seeing ourselves as an innocent bystander in our failed relationships is a measure of our own immaturity. In the same way that addiction led us to repeat old patterns, the pain we experience in relationships keeps reopening old wounds. When we don't acknowledge these unhealed wounds and we do something to reopen them (such as becoming emotionally vulnerable), they fester or break open again.

To protect ourselves, we become hyper-vigilant, just waiting for the next uncomfortable moment with a partner to reinforce our negative expectations. Then we believe the other person "forces" us to do what we do. We develop a knee-jerk response based on our negative expectations. We push back every time there is an imagined shove. We develop our reactiveness in an attempt to keep ourselves out of harm's way. We think the presence of pain means somebody screwed up. More often than not, however, we accidentally open the scars on our old wounds as we try to get closer to one another. No one is to blame.

It takes time and maturity to be able to identify and interrupt our participation in creating more of what we don't want. It would be unrealistic to expect angry or depressed adolescents to see clearly how their actions invite responses that drive the knife deeper into their tender psyches. Even as adults, we are so obsessed with the pain, we cannot see anything behind it. (Remember the cycle of stress.) We have to work hard to assess fairly the way the events that led up to a hurtful moment unfolded, and what we did to contribute. It takes considerable effort—when the pressure of a conflict is bearing down on us—to not assassinate the other person's character or our own.

How to Keep from Re-creating Your Worst Fears

With our unhealed wounds newly exposed in a relationship, we have a built-in distortion (an over-reaction or under-reaction during conflict) that needs to be calmly identified and examined. Self-reflection, or "checking in" on our over-reactions and under-reactions, is essential to figuring out if these old wounds are still active, or if we have dealt with them sufficiently so we're not driven to travel the old brain pathways of duck and cover—fight or flight.

Because of the difficulty of making a mature, balanced assessment of who did what to whom, some people lock on to their old standby self-image—that is, the angry or depressed victim role they developed when they were younger. As a result, they never grow up. They remain hopelessly adolescent in their approach to intimate relationships. Their self-fulfilling prophecies continue to operate right under their noses without a glimmer of recognition.

If we believe that we aren't going to be able to handle things, and that life serves up lots of overwhelming events, it isn't long before we start feeling overwhelmed. If we think the world is out to get us and we react aggressively, then the people approaching us have their guard up. This "forces" us to acquire and use "lethal weapons" to protect ourselves from people whose reactiveness and defensiveness we had a hand in creating. We project meaning away from ourselves and see events happening *to* us. In that way, our own defensiveness can kick into gear and protect us from harm without the slightest self-examination. We are on automatic pilot, acting on a self-reinforcing loop of our own creation. The three knee-jerk reactions—blaming you, blaming me, or blaming both of us—are activated, and we punish our perpetrators severely.

For example, Diane had been feeling amorous all day, but even though she repeatedly gave Brian subtle hints as evening approached, he hadn't seemed to show the slightest interest in getting intimate. She was starting to feel invisible. In addition, she had put on a few pounds since summer. Lately, she'd begun to feel kind of slovenly when she looked in the mirror. The voice of self-criticism was becoming harder and harder to block out. The fear of becoming unattractive, especially when she compared herself to all the women she saw on TV, sapped more of her sense of herself as a woman. Here, however, she was about to create her worst fear.

Diane: Brian, I don't understand. I've been trying all day long to get a rise out of you, but you've been acting like I don't even exist. What's wrong? And what does a girl have to do to get a little love around here?

Brian: Hey, it's finally football season, and you know how much I enjoy watching it. Boring old baseball isn't clogging up the channels anymore, so give me a break, will ya please? I'm in hog heaven.

Diane: Are you sure you're not just getting bored with me? Maybe the honeymoon is over since I've put on a little extra weight. You have noticed, haven't you?

Brian: It really isn't a big deal, hon. Yeah, I've noticed your jeans are getting kinda snug, but that doesn't make me love you any less. I haven't said anything about it because I didn't want you to get sensitive on me. I simply have more of you to love. I think of myself as a bigger and bigger landowner, that's all. I'm really a very lucky guy.

Diane: I knew it, I just knew it! How long have you been feeling this way about my weight? I could tell it was bothering you all along.

Does this scenario sound familiar to you? If so, when and with whom? Are there several relationships where this or another self-fulfilling prophecy has played out? Let's look at this same scenario played out differently using several of the Big Ideas and tools we've learned in this book.

Brian, for example, could stand still in the moment, dig deeper into what Diane is truly feeling, and collaborate with an agreement to meet her need once the game is over. He could acknowledge the truth of whatever she feels about her weight issue. He could help her dig deeper and cultivate confusion about what's going on between them. There could be several scripts in her life playing out here, such as a script from childhood when one or more family members considered her "plump" and thus, in Diane's mind, she will always be plump. Could this be a script that Diane still carries and brings into her relationship with Brian?

On Diane's part, it becomes clear that she's someone who turns her blame inward. A self-fulfilling prophecy occurred when she imagined that the criticism she subjected herself to was the same criticism that everyone else, including Brian, silently shared. She went looking for an explanation to make sense of Brian's inattentiveness. She projected her interpretation onto a blank screen. She put words in Brian's mouth, and then turned his innocent response into proof positive that her weight had been keeping them apart.

What Are Your Self-Fulfilling Prophecies?

- What are your self-fulfilling prophecies, and how do they seem to work in your life?
- Look at the anticipations and expectations that you carry.
- Some are beliefs—like *"I will never amount to anything."*
- Our fears tell us to expect the worst; and when they happen, we may not notice the role we played in bringing these into our lives.

It takes effort at first to not project your preconceived notions into a conflict situation. By using several of the Big Ideas, Diane could collect new information about her partner, and also about herself. She could work out of her intellect to resolve and influence the behavior of Brian by suggesting they collaborate on finding a solution that is mutually satisfying. One suggestion is that she could do something for herself while he is watching the game, with an agreement that they will come together after that point to cuddle and visit. Instead, she proceeded in a way that mirrored her own self-criticism back at her.

There are many other scripts that we believe about ourselves (often given to us by others) that have played out repeatedly in our lives. We tend to focus on the negative scripts and believe them more each time they reoccur. This reinforces the belief that we are chained to them for life! We believe that we have no power to change. We are not innocent bystanders in life unless we choose to be. It is your life, and once you begin to acknowledge the negative and unproductive scripts that play in your mind, the sooner you can change and heal. When we do not take the lead to change, we continue to suffer these feelings, and the pain breaks open the wounds we were trying to heal. If this happens over and over again, we become hyper-vigilant and are constantly waiting for the other shoe to drop in our relationships. When we hear something that is familiar to the script that is negative, we make an automatic knee-jerk reaction—that most often is an over-reaction. We no longer have control of our emotions; our limbic has control of those emotions that are caused by either our own scripts or someone else's that we have kept as our own.

Befriending the Cortex to Make Change Happen

The internal power that we have to change old scripts is great once we learn to use our cortex. Without it we are impulsive reactors. Instead, we can choose who we are and how we are by the way we think and behave. Taking a fearless inventory of the scripts by which we live, then deciding if these are the scripts we want to keep, is an essential first step. Others include confiding in someone you trust, flushing out the negative, and talking back to the limbic when it rears up with criticism and doubt.

Looking thoroughly at yourself as you currently are, and deciding which behavioral changes are essential to obtaining healthier and happier relationships, helps secure the pathways in your cortex into a new thought pattern—a pattern that will eventually become a habit.

Your cortex is the tool that will help you live in the *we* and not the *me*. Remind yourself that this is *the* way to change yourself and the responses of others around you. Remember that this change starts with you. You have the power to change yourself! You have the power to affect others! It is up to you how your new script is played out.

Changing Our Scripts

- It takes time and maturity to identify and interrupt these attitudes and thoughts.
- We must work hard to fairly assess the events leading up to hurtful moments.
- We must make an effort not to assassinate the other person's character or our own.
- We must calmly identify and examine our internal distortions.
- An adolescent approach to intimate relationships will result in the self-fulfilling prophecy of relationships never working out!

Conflict, fighting, and disagreement are integral parts of life. Without them, little would consciously change or improve. Peaceful coexistence or collaboration is not achieved through repressing our natural human emotions or through forced or artificial tranquility. It is achieved by exploring our feelings and issues honestly and openly without hurting another in the process. It happens by agreeing to look at our own scripts and rewrite what is no longer helpful or healthy. I wonder what your script will look like as you reflect on the changes you want to make? Maybe it is time to rein in your own brain and decide what you want to change. Please see How Will I Rein In My Brain? in appendix A and consider just what you need to help you control your limbic brain.

Thank you so much for reading and being a part of this learning process to rein in your brain! Applying the Ten Big Ideas in my own life has changed the way I live, the way I raised my children, and my personal and work relationships. As a way to live, it sure beats anything I did before completely embracing these ideas.

I will close this book with the phrase "up to this time." I suggest that you write your own "up-to-this-time" life script. Up to this time in your life, you did whatever it is that you did. You may have fought too much, accommodated too much, avoided too much, and, of course, allowed your limbic brain to have its way too much. Your life choices are really *only* up to you now. Now you have the opportunity to change them and start each day anew, with different thoughts and behaviors that will change your brain and enable you to live more thoughtfully in recovery.

Many blessings as you move through your life. It is yours to change and influence!

Cynthia's Self-Fulfilling Prophecy—Busted

My last case manager told me, as I ended my senior year of high school, that I could not go to college to become a social worker. This was the dream I had—to become educated and help others who had life stories like mine. She told me I was not smart enough. She also said that since I had "used up" tax money all my life as a ward of the court, the state would only agree to spend money to send me to school for a one-year clerical certificate program at the local community college. That was not my dream! When

I went home and recounted this to my foster parents, Ann and Dwight, they made an appointment with the supervisor of this caseworker. At the appointed time and date we went in to see this supervisor—as a team. Ann and Dwight stated my case. They acknowledged that my grades were not super. However, they pointed to the improvement made since I had been in their home. They also pointed out my involvement with youth clubs and activities through which I'd reached out to help others, including my church youth group, high school girls club, and dance team.

I could hardly believe what happened next. The supervisor said that I could go to college with state support as a ward of the court *if* (and this seemed like a big *if* at the time) I kept my grades up. My life script and all the wounds that lay beneath it were busted that day. Through their actions and words, Ann and Dwight taught me how to speak the language of possibilities to others so that they, like me, would hear. It was my first lesson in advocacy, a skill set that became my life's work.

_____

Lifelong Changes Using the Ten Big Ideas

Use the table below to record the lifelong behavior changes you plan to make. Next to the behavior changes, indicate the tips, strategies, and/or methods you plan to use from the Ten Big Ideas.

Behaviors to Change	Big Idea: Tools, Strategies, and Methods

APPENDIX A

How Will I Rein In My Brain?

Hear it: What words/phrases do I need to hear?

_____

_____

_____

_____

_____

See it: What words/phrases do I need to see and how can I see them (sticky notes on the mirror or refrigerator)?

_____

_____

_____

_____

_____

Say it: What words/phrases do I need to be saying to myself and others—over and over?

_____

_____

_____

_____

_____

Write it: What words/phrases do I need to write?

_____

_____

_____

_____

_____

Read it: What words/phrases do I need to read several times a day?

_____

_____

_____

_____

_____

Repeat it: When can I practice these words/phrases and where?

_____

_____

_____

_____

_____

APPENDIX B

Phrases That Come
from the Cortex

It is possible . . . ?

Have you had an opportunity to . . . ?

I wonder what would happen if . . . ?

Help me understand.

I'm confused. I thought . . .

Is this okay with you?

I'm curious about . . .

Please explain to me . . .

It would be my pleasure to . . .

Please.

Thank you.

May I have permission to . . . ?

Please tell me what you mean by . . .

When you have a minute, would you please . . . ?

I am sorry.

Is there another way I could (say this, explain this, etc.)?

Let us discover (consider, believe, etc.) . . .

Often, this is a misunderstood (action, behavior, word, etc.).

It could be . . .

Another possibility is . . .

Another way to look at it is . . .

What about this idea?

Let's consider . . .

Will you agree to . . . ?

I would like to find a solution together.

Would you consider . . . ?

I would like to assist you.

I feel _____ when _____ occurs, and then I want to _____.

I request _____ instead.

About the Authors

Cynthia Moreno Tuohy, BSW, NCAC II, is the executive director of NAADAC, the Association for Addiction Professionals. She previously served as the executive director of Danya Institute and the Central East Addiction Technology Transfer Center. Prior to this she was the program director for Volunteers of America–Western Washington, serving homeless populations and dealing with the co-occurrence of poverty and substance abuse issues. She has also written training components and manuals about working with adolescents, adults, and seniors; school intervention; involuntary commitment; community mobilization; intensive outpatient treatment and continuing care; the foundations of addiction practice; medication-assisted recovery; impaired driver programs; employee assistance programs; and gang intervention and treatment.

Victoria Costello is an Emmy Award–winning science journalist who has established a national platform through her publishing and advocacy work in mental health and wellness. In January 2012, she released her memoir, *A Lethal Inheritance: A Mother Uncovers the Science behind Three Generations of Mental Illness.* Her co-authored works include *The Complete Idiot's Guide to Child &*

Adolescent Psychology (2011), written with child psychiatrist Jack C. Westman, M.D., M.S.; *The Complete Idiot's Guide to the Chemistry of Love* (2010), written with evolutionary psychologist Maryanne Fisher; *The Everything Parent's Guide to Children with OCD;* and *The Everything Guide to a Happy Marriage,* both written with Stephen Martin, M.F.T.

Hazelden, a national nonprofit organization founded in 1949, helps people reclaim their lives from the disease of addiction. Built on decades of knowledge and experience, Hazelden offers a comprehensive approach to addiction that addresses the full range of patient, family, and professional needs, including treatment and continuing care for youth and adults, research, higher learning, public education and advocacy, and publishing.

A life of recovery is lived "one day at a time." Hazelden publications, both educational and inspirational, support and strengthen lifelong recovery. In 1954, Hazelden published *Twenty-Four Hours a Day,* the first daily meditation book for recovering alcoholics, and Hazelden continues to publish works to inspire and guide individuals in treatment and recovery, and their loved ones. Professionals who work to prevent and treat addiction also turn to Hazelden for evidence-based curricula, informational materials, and videos for use in schools, treatment programs, and correctional programs.

Through published works, Hazelden extends the reach of hope, encouragement, help, and support to individuals, families, and communities affected by addiction and related issues.

For questions about Hazelden publications,
please call **800-328-9000** or
visit us online at **hazelden.org/bookstore.**

Other titles that may interest you:

Craving
Why We Can't Seem to Get Enough
OMAR MANEJWALA, M.D.

A nationally recognized expert on compulsive behaviors explains the phenomenon of craving and gives us tools to achieve freedom from our seemingly insatiable desires by changing our actions to remap our brains.
Order No. 4677 (softcover), EB4677 (e-book)

12 Stupid Things That Mess Up Recovery
Avoiding Relapse through Self-Awareness and Right Action
ALLEN BERGER, PH.D.

Berger explores the twelve most commonly confronted beliefs and attitudes that can sabotage recovery, and then provides tools for working through these problems in daily life.
Order No. 3001 (softcover), EB3001 (e-book)

12 Smart Things to Do When the Booze and Drugs Are Gone
Choosing Emotional Sobriety through Self-Awareness and Right Action
ALLEN BERGER, PH.D.

Berger draws on the teachings of Bill W. and psychotherapy pioneers to offer twelve hallmarks of emotional sobriety that, when practiced, give people the confidence to be accountable for their behavior, ask for what they want and need, and grow and develop a deeper trust in the process of life.
Order No. 2864 (softcover), EB2864 (e-book)

Hazelden books are available at fine bookstores everywhere.
To order from Hazelden, call **800-328-9000**
or visit **hazelden.org/bookstore.**